layla Audeamus

SURRENDER

ISBN: 979-8-88945-028-3
eISBN: 979-8-88945-029-0

Brilliant Books Literary
137 Forest Park Lane Thomasville
North Carolina 27360 USA

Printed in the United States of America

ACKNOWLEDGEMENTS

For a dear, sweet friend who helped to steer me in the right direction;
The loves who are no longer here but the one who came and rescued me from a formless, Masterless existence, I've given my body, behavior, and attitude and you accepted.

SUB-TO-BE

L ittle Alice, David looked down at the kneeling, naked girl who had just asked if he would accept her as his sub. The apprehension he'd felt that he would have to release this girl that he loved was lifted from his shoulders. In his mind he was forming his response but, in his heart, he was shouting at the joy he knew she would bring to his life.

He lifted her chin and bade her look at him. "I will be pleased to accept you as my sub once your initial training is complete." He pulled her into his lap and hugged and kissed her.

David wanted to stay the night with her but because of patient appointments he would need to stay at his condo in order to make the first ones scheduled. He told her to finish in the kitchen and go to the master bedroom to prepare for bed. He returned the cane he had used on her to the dungeon and wanted to change.

In the bedroom Alice waited for David to do the nightly inspection. With her legs far apart and bent at the waist over the end of the bed, her pussy and ass were in full view to be examined and for David to decide how he might want to use her. Tonight, however, he simply gave her a couple of smacks with his hand on her butt. "From now on I want you to wear the heavy leather collar in the house full time and when you are in bed. You will continue to sleep with the right ankle cuff attached to the bed."

He walked Alice to the room where she would sleep and locked the leather collar in place. "After we are married, there will be a formal collaring ceremony. I will choose a collar for you to wear. Remember, it is and always will be my collar. If you need to take this one off to shower, the key is on the night stand, but it goes back on as soon as possible. Also, it is only to be worn in the house, but don't let me come home and find you with a bare neck." He tucked in his girl, kissed her, and turned out the light. "I will call you before I come home tomorrow."

Alice lay in the darkened room and ran her hand over the collar and the padlock David had secured to her neck. She felt a peace envelope her she hadn't known for a long time. Tomorrow she was going to sign a short-term lease on the office space she liked and when she came home, she would shed her vanilla, outside self, and take up her place as David's, Sir's, sub-to-be.

She would have to work at remembering that in the house or a lifestyle setting David would be called Sir but in public he would either be David or if non-attention provoking, Sir. There were certain areas of her life, mainly having to do with the estate and her personal finances, she would continue to be responsible for but in her life with Sir, she was giving him control because she didn't want it. She knew he would always act in their best interests and keep her safe.

The office space was a good idea. She knew that she must keep up contact with friends and take care of her business interests. There was also a charity she was interested in but before she committed to it, she wanted to discuss it with Sir.

Alice parked the Shelby in the garage and took the fresh bread she had bought into the house. The first place she went was to the place she had made for herself in the corner of her bedroom, her Zen space, where she could change from her 'outside' self to her 'inside' self. Hanging up her suit and changing her heels for the soft slippers she had been told to wear in the house, she concentrated on the commitment she was making to Sir and to their relationship. "I am freely giving myself; body, behavior, and attitude to Sir. I give him control over me in all things. He is my Sir and will guide me, teach me, train me in his vision, and punish me when necessary. He is my Sir." The mantra ran though her head and at times she whispered it to herself. After she felt prepared to go about her duties at home as a sub, she left the room and began preparing the dinner she would give her Sir.

Alice put some light background music on as she finished up the dinner. She had learned that the life of a surgeon was not strictly a nine-to-five. It was not unusual for her to have to keep dinner far beyond the usual time in order to accommodate his schedule. Tonight, was just such a night.

Alice passed the extra time looking over some of the proposals the bank had sent over regarding her investments. One of the gentlemen she knew at the bank had been a friend of her parent's and had guided her mother through the investment maze her father had left her when he died. She sent an email to him and asked if she might have a meeting with him sometime in the next week or so.

The last time she had seen George Nolan was at her mother's funeral. He had sent some flowers to Aunt Dorie's funeral but didn't attend. Alice figured he must be close to retirement age and hoped she would have a chance to at least talk to him before he was put out to graze. It surprised her then when she got an immediate reply and an invitation to lunch the next Wednesday at the Breakers Club at one o'clock. She quickly accepted. Now she would just have to tell Sir about the lunch and remind him of it on the day and it was all set.

Alice's phone chirped with a text message from David that he was on his way home. She quickly checked the dinner, put everything away she had been doing, and took her formal greeting position at the door. Just thinking about Sir coming through the door so that she could greet him made her quiver in anticipation.

David's heart warmed when he saw Alice prostrate in the kowtow position he had taught her. He put his keys and case on the table then turned and told his girl to kneel before him. "Suck it" he said as he pulled his cock from his pants.

With a big smile on her face, she quickly got into a kneeling position before him and began to lick, suck, and pull his full cock deeper and deeper down her throat. She enjoyed doing this for him and looked forward to her prize of his cum filling her mouth. As he got closer and closer to coming, David took both of his hands and held her head steady while he fucked her mouth. With some deep guttural sounds he came and Alice swallowed his cum. She licked him clean before he put his spent cock back into his pants.

"I look forward to the day when you will be doing that when I first wakeup in the mornings." He lifted her to a standing position and looked her up and down. He kissed her and then told her to go and put the meal on. Before she left though he whispered in her ear, "I'm going to enjoy using you tonight my pet."

Alice hurried to the kitchen and put the food on the table and cut the fresh bread to go with it. During dinner David asked her about her day and she told him about the office space and the lunch the old family friend, George Nolan. had invited her to on the next Wednesday.

David went to his room to change and told Alice to finish cleaning the kitchen and then meet him in the dungeon. Alice was wet with anticipation of what David was going to do to her. When she entered the dungeon, he was holding a leather leash.

"I want to teach you how to walk with me. When I put this leash on, it also means you can't speak. If we were to go to a lifestyle event and had you on a leash, no one would be speaking to you because they would know you were on speech restriction. If you see someone on a leash, assume that is also for restricting that person's speech." David snapped the leash onto the O ring on the heavy collar she was wearing and he led her around the room.

Fifteen minutes later he removed the leash and asked Alice to walk with him. She kept the correct distance and as he gave her several scenarios in which they might find themselves, she was able to act properly for each. He was pleased with her progress so far but she still had some way to go.

He sat down on the sofa and told Alice to kneel in front of him. He gave her a cushion from the couch to kneel on so her knees would not hurt and she lowered her eyes as he had instructed her do when he first taught her this position. "Are you still happy with your decision to become my sub, Alice?"

"Yes, Sir" she said.

David reached out and raised her head. "I think that when I ask you to speak and you are in this position you should look me in the eyes." She raised her head. "So, you're happy about this?" She again said she was. "Alice, on Sunday afternoon, when I know there will be no workers on the site, I will take you to see the new house I am building. Would you like that?"

"Yes, Sir" Alice said.

"Good, it is far enough along that I think it would give you an idea of where we will be living once it is complete." Alice was intrigued. She had known he was having a house built, but he had never told her anything more and it was not her place to ask.

David stood and put the leash away. Turning, he told her to go to the master bedroom so he could do the inspection. He was tired and he was going to leave any further play in the dungeon until the weekend. Alice had been looking forward to more than just some leash training but knew it wasn't up to her, but to Sir to decide these things.

Friday night was a special occasion for David and Alice. It would be the first time David could fuck Alice without having to use a condom. The two didn't speak about it, but each had been counting the days until the contraception was supposed to be effective at preventing his girl from getting pregnant. Alice hoped David would want to use her but she knew he would be the one to make that decision, not her. On Friday morning early, David called Alice to tell her he would call her before he was coming home and to prepare to be used in the dungeon. "I will bring dinner, you just prepare to be used," David said.

All day Alice thought about what she had been told. Shortly after mid-day Alice received a text message from David with instructions on preparing her ass to be used. She went to the bathroom and did as she was told. The closer it got to David's time to come home, the wetter she got with the anticipation. Finally, the message from David that he was on his way home and expected to be greeted properly.

Alice was in the kowtow position when she heard David's step on the front porch and his key in the lock. He said nothing as he came in the house but Alice stayed exactly as she was and would keep that position until David told her to do otherwise. She heard him drop his bag and keys on the table and heard him turn.

David walked in the kitchen and left his girl in the foyer. She could hear the sounds of plastic bags being set on the counter and opened. Finally, her prospective Sir came back to the front door. "Stand and greet me girl."

Alice rose and gave David the formal hug he'd taught her and he kissed her forehead. "Come, we will eat while it is hot." Two plates and the necessary things were put on the table and they ate their meal. David asked her about her day and told her about his. The plates went into the dishwasher and the empty take-out boxes were rinsed and put in the trash.

"I want you in the dungeon now." David left the kitchen and made his way down the hall. Inside he changed to his tee-shirt and jeans, Alice was told to stand by the spanking/fucking bench. David put a blindfold on her, attached the cuffs and collar to the restraint points on the bench, and then he put a small butt plug in Alice's ass.

Although he had put some lubricant on the plug, it was difficult to insert. He smiled when he saw the sheen of oil he'd told Alice to use earlier in the day and that she was to reapply each time she used the toilet. Once the plug was in, he turned it around a few times and noticed how it elicited a moaning response from Alice.

"From now on, I want you to always keep your ass ready for me to use it if I want. We must train your ass to use bigger and bigger butt-plugs until it will be both comfortable and pleasurable for you when I use it. The lube I told you to use will make it easier on you but if you forget it, that is on you, I will use it anyway even if it might be painful for you." David stepped away from her and chose a flogger from those hanging on the wall.

The music was like the instrumental guitar, but a longer version that would give David time to really work on his girl before a climax. After the flogger he switched to his old leather belt which raised a row of welts on her ass. Each time he hit the butt-plug Alice could feel it inside of her and it was new and pleasurable. The music was building and David changed to his hand. As the beat of the song was reaching a crescendo, he took his fully erect and engorged cock from his pants and entered Alice without a condom.

He could look down and see his cock moving in and out of her, a sight that gave him so much joy and excited him even more. From his back pocket he pulled a mini vibrator. He put it on high and licked the ball on the end of it. With one hand he found Alice's clit and put the vibrator on it. Immediately her body began to react to the stimulus. "David," she screamed, "fuck me David, fuck me." David felt her explode into a body-arching orgasm as his cum shot into her vagina. He removed the vibrator and tossed it onto the sofa. He stayed in her as the last of the waves coursed through her. As he pulled out, his thick, milky-white cum rolled out of his girl. Moving to her head he put his cock in her mouth so she could lick it clean.

David released her restraints and removed the blindfold. He put her in his lap on the sofa and held her as they both recovered from the effects of their play. The last thing to do was remove the butt-plug. More than an hour after they finished on the bench, David finally told Alice to go up to the master bedroom so they could pre-pare to go to bed.

"I will be sleeping here tonight and I want you to stay in the bed with me. I've got somethings to do in here and then I'll be up and I expect you to be in the formal inspection position at the foot of the bed." David turned to wipe down the vibrator, butt-plug, and spanking bench while Alice left to do as she was told.

Alice was bent over the foot of the bed, waiting for David as he came into the master bedroom. Her ass was still red and the welts were visible. He admired his handiwork while he changed to pajama pants. "From now on, I want you to use a butt-plug during the day while you are home. I've put a small silicone plug in the bathroom which you will begin with. I have bigger ones as you ass getting looser. Just be aware that I may want to use your ass at any time so you will have the oil I told you to use on it all the time and reapply it after each time you use the toilet. Keep a small bottle of it in your purse and some wet wipes also. Even if you are outside of the house, I want that oil on."

"Tonight, you are going to sleep in this bed with me. But you will also learn a valuable lesson. You will be bound to this bed, not just with one ankle, but with both and your hands will also both be bound. I want you to feel what your commitment to me is all about and it will also demonstrate that it is not all flogging, spanking, and fucking." She needed to know that what they just did in the dungeon was the exception and not the norm. Life in a D/s lifestyle was about the living together not just the playing together.

He told her to get on the bed so he could secure the ropes to her ankle and wrist cuffs. David kissed her on the forehead and covered her up to her waist with the sheet and blanket. He pulled each one of her nipples before turning out the light on the nightstand. She heard him move around to the other side of the bed and felt his weight on it when he got in. He turned out the light and within minutes she heard his breathing slow as he slipped into sleep.

Alice lay in the dark and tried to find a comfortable position in which to sleep. She had always thought that the first night she could sleep with David they would be entwined in each other's arms but she understood his lesson. Finally, as the large red numerals on the alarm clock turned to midnight, she slipped off into sleep.

Early in the morning David took the restraints off of Alice so she could get up and go to the bathroom. He told her to come back to bed, she had a service to fulfill. Returning to the bed, she saw the covers completely off the bed and David laying with nothing on and his cock was fully erect. "Kneel down on the bed and suck it." She did as he instructed and quickly had him ready to climax. He pulled out of her mouth and got behind her. He slipped his cock into Alice and shot his cum into her. "Stay as you are. I want to take a picture of the cum rolling out of you."

"I won't always finish your morning duty like this, mostly you will just suck my cock until I cum in your mouth and you will swallow it. Do you think you can remember that?" Alice told him she was happy to do that. "Good, I also want you to leave the cum alone until you take your shower. I like seeing your bare thighs glisten with my cum." He stood up and reached for his pajama pants. "Get to the kitchen and make our breakfast before you shower." Alice went to the kitchen and began the day.

Showered and the oil applied as David had requested, Alice put the butt-plug in her he'd left in the bathroom. It felt a little strange but as she moved around the house or sat at the computer to work, she realized she didn't notice it was there.

David had gone to the hospital to check on a patient who was being released and called just before noon to tell Alice he would be home soon. "I want you to be at the door for me and then we need to talk," he said.

Alice greeted David at the door as usual and he told her to go to the kitchen. He had several things he put in the fridge, telling her they were for Sunday. She put the lunch on the table as directed and once they had finished eating and Alice had cleared and cleaned the kitchen, he had her sit at the table.

"Tomorrow we will go see the new house," David started, "it is supposed to be done in about six months so we don't have much time to finish your training before I want to move into it. Because of that, we have been invited to a lifestyle friend's house this evening. We will go and I want you to be on the leash. I don't want you to speak, but you are going to listen and watch what other subs and slaves do. You will also get a chance to see other masters and observe how they treat and interact with their own subs/slaves and with others."

He continued, "I will pick out something for you to wear. You will not wear panties or a bra but will have your butt-plug in." Alice wondered about the butt-plug, but was comfortable going without the bra and panties.

David stayed at the table and Alice felt he had something else to say to her. She didn't have long to wait, "tell me your thoughts. We have spent our first full night together, we are playing more in the dungeon, and you have asked to be my sub; do you regret your decision or wish to slow down? I'm not a mind reader and I want to know how you feel."

Alice looked at David, she had made the decision to give herself to him and she would not change that. Was she happy about the play or anything else? She knew why she had spent the last night bound, she may not have liked it, but it wasn't for her to like or not. "Sir, I feel wonderful, a bit sore, but I wouldn't change my decision at all."

He kissed her on the forehead as he got up from the table. "Good, then let's get you dressed!"

In the bedroom Alice used, David rummaged through her closets until he found a very short skirt and an almost sheer blouse. Alice was worried about bending over in the skirt and without a bra on, nothing of her breasts would be left to the imagination. She was told to try the items on and David had her curtsy, bow, and stand in various positions. He changed the skirt for an equally short one but it did cover her better as she walked.

"Do you wonder about the clothes I've chosen for you pet?" David asked.

Alice stood before him and said it was for him to choose what she wore. "Exactly! It is for me to choose but I don't think I want anyone else getting such a full view of my girl, so you will put on the black dress that is laying out for you on the bed in the master bedroom. Go put it on and let's see it."

Alice took the skirt and blouse off, hung them in the closet and retrieved the dress David had laid out on the other bed. It fit her like a second skin. Every curve was accentuated and her nipples were prominent. It was mid-calf in length with a slit up the front and the back was open to her waist. The front also dropped into a deep V.

A bit of two-sided tape, the kind runway models used, was applied to keep the front from causing a wardrobe malfunction when she bowed, curtsied, or knelt in the dress. It was perfect with the stiletto heels David asked her to wear. David sent Alice off to change, shower and prepare for the party. They would leave at seven and he wanted her to be on time.

She was waiting for him at the foot of the stairs as he came down in a black silk shirt, black trousers, and a pair of highly polished boots. He put a black jacket on and helped Alice into her coat. He gave her the heavy collar to carry and he had the leash wrapped around his waist. He would put them on Alice when they got to the party.

"The people you will be meeting tonight are a very diverse group," David told her as he was driving to Oakland. "My group is made up of M/s or D/s male owning female couples but this is kind of demo is usually people of all kinds. There is going to be a demonstration tonight by a Mistress Jordan who owns several slaves, both male and female, about fisting. You will also see some same-sex couples and many who are not in relationships. The demo is in a private home, someone I've known for years, who is no longer active but has a great dungeon and loves to host these kinds of events."

"Your behavior," David continued, "will reflect upon me so I caution you to remember all you have learned. Don't speak unless I remove the leash and give you permission." He reached over and tweaked a nipple, "remember, I love you and I'm proud of you. I want you to do very well. Listen, learn, and observe."

David stopped before a house not dissimilar from the old house where Alice now lived except it was much larger. Two couple were going in the front door and light spilled across the porch before the door closed behind them. The two gas lanterns flanking the massive front door were the only light against the darkness of the night. David parked and when he helped Alice out, he put the collar on her and unwound the leash from his waist and snapped it in place. He gave Alice a kiss on the forehead and led her up the steps to the door.

The owner of the house and their host greeted David and smiled at Alice. "So, is this the girl you have been telling me about?" he inquired. The man introduced himself as Master Morris. He was probably in his late sixties, had graying hair and mustache, and stood only about five feet nine. His penetrating ice-blue eyes took in every detail and Alice had the feeling of being a newly captured butterfly under his expert gaze. "She is a fine-looking one, I'll give you that."

Alice had dropped into a deep curtsy and a slight movement of the leash told her to rise. She stood with eyes downcast until another slight sign from David indicated he wanted her to look directly at their host. Another couple appeared at the door and Master Morris turned his attention toward them.

David walked into the giant room off the entry and found a place to sit in the long rows of chairs facing the front of the room where the demo would be done. He motioned for Alice to put her bag across the chairs in order to save them for later. Next, they went back into the foyer and turned into another room where several people were milling around and visiting with each other.

A tall black man dressed in leathers from head to boots stood with a petite blond girl who was very pregnant. Dressed in a short skirt whose waist was under her belly and a top that barely covered her huge tits much less the rest of her, the girl teetered on high heels that looked out of place with the rest of her appearance.

"Master Robert," David greeted the man, "your slave looks almost ready to pop! How far along is she?"

Robert smiled and patted his slave's belly, "She's going to give me a son just about any day now. I brought her out tonight because this will probably be her last outing before the midwife comes to deliver baby number four. The three little girls are home with my other slave, rehanna. She's not due to drop her baby until next month, but it's a girl too."

Robert looked closer at Alice. "A good-looking girl you've got there. How far along in training is she?"

David smiled, "she will be ready when I formally collar her in about six months." Robert and David shook hands and David led Alice to another group.

A small woman dressed in thigh-high, sharp heeled boots, black leather corset, and black skirt stood holding the leashes of a girl of about eighteen and a young man who was not much older. The girl was in a shift dress, much like the one Alice had at home that she had been instructed to wear if anyone besides David was with them in the house, and the young man wore nothing but a loin cloth.

David greeted the woman as Mistress Jordan. "It's been a long time since I've seen you! How have you been?"

"Oh David, it has been a while, hasn't it. I suppose you still aren't interested in joining my house? Hm, didn't think so, but I had to ask." Mistress Jordan laughed and caressed David's hand. "So, you have yourself a new girl! Interesting. Are you training her or looking to trade her? I wouldn't give up my lilly, but maybe little peter would do okay for you." She pulled the leash of the young man, "show David what you are hiding under your skirt."

The one named peter pulled his loincloth aside to reveal his cock and balls encased in a stainless-steel cage. "I keep him under tight control so he doesn't get any ideas."

David shook his head, "Mistress Jordan I'm not interested in a trade and wouldn't have anything I could do with your boy. Best you keep him in your house."

Mistress Jordan laughed. "he's got small hands and is excellent at fisting. He will be demonstrating on lilly a little later. Do you want him to show you how to fist your girl? I'm sure he would like to do it to her."

David moved Alice so she was standing behind him, "No, I'm good. Fisting is something I will do myself when the time comes, but I do want to see your slaves do the demo."

Alice was happy to move on to the next couple to which David led her. The man was a little older than David and at his side was a lady who looked to be about the same age as Alice. David introduced the man as Master Phillip and his slave louise. The slave curtsied to David just as Alice did to Master Phillip. Louise smiled at Alice but observed the fact she wasn't allowed to speak.

Master Phillip asked David what Alice might like to drink and told his slave to get a white wine for Alice and an ice tea for David. Alice watched as the slave did as she was told and was pleased to see the beautiful way she moved. Everything she did reminded Alice of calmness and assurance in who and what she was. Alice looked into David's eyes and wished she could be like louise. Master Phillip watched his girl with such pleasure in his eyes and he was proud of the way she moved.

When louise returned with the drinks the two couples stood so the men could have a chance to visit. Alice heard herself referenced a couple of times and Master Phillip was telling David that louise was in her first trimester of pregnancy.

"Congratulations, do you know what she's carrying yet?" David asked. "This is the first time you've bred her so it's kind of a big deal!"

Master Phillip caressed louise's' belly. "I had her taking her temperature every day and we hit it on the second try. So far, we just know she is doing okay but we will find out the sex next week. I expect a boy but I'll take whatever I put in her." Alice noticed the smile on louise's face as her Master beamed over her.

Everyone started to move toward the big room so the demo could get underway. The girl in the shift had been placed, naked, on a table at the head of the room and on an adjacent table two glass bowls sat next to a stack of towels. Mistress Jordan stood next to the girl and peter next to the bowls on the table.

"This is my girl, lilly. She is going to be the demo doll tonight and peter will be doing the demo while I narrate." Mistress Jordan nodded to peter who picked up one of the bowls to show a gelatinous white mass in it. "This is the lubricant that we use. It is hypo-allergenic and safe to be used on humans. Now peter will coat the hand he will use when he fists lilly with it."

Peter put his hand in the goop and ran the gelatin through his fingers. Next, he pulled his hand out and put his hand up. "Now he will show you how to hold your hand." Peter made his fingers look almost like a duck's bill with all of the fingers and thumb coming to a point. "You see how it looks? This is what you want."

She turned to peter who took some of the goop out of the bowl and put on lilly's pussy. lilly lay on the table with her knees bent and spread wide so her genitals were on display for all to see. "Now, carefully, peter will begin to work his hand into her pussy. There will be some resistance, especially as you get to the pubic ridge, but once you work your way past that," she looked over at peter, "are you all the way in?" Peter continued to work his way into lilly.

Peter nodded to his Mistress. "Excellent. You feel the cervix?" Peter nodded again. "Now, find the g-spot and bring her to climax! She deserves something for her cooperation tonight!" Peter soon had lilly writhing on the table in an orgasm. He pulled his hand out and rinsed it in the water of the second bowl. He took a towel, dipped it in the water, and used it to clean the goop off of lilly and dried her with another towel. Finally, Mistress Jordan told lilly she could get down but not to put her dress back on.

There were questions from many of those in attendance and others simply stood around and talked. There were some snacks on the table, but David decided it was time for them to leave. After goodbyes were said, David led Alice to the front porch where he took off the leash and undid the collar.

In the car David kissed Alice. "You did very well for your first outing. How do you feel? Any questions about what you saw or people you met?"

Alice was full of questions and they talked on the way home. "I enjoyed myself and I hope we can go out again, but I also would like to get to know louise better. I think she and I might be friends if her Master and you will allow it."

David was pleased. "I would like that. Her Master is part of my circle of friends and they will be seen at most of the functions we will attend as a couple." David pulled into the driveway of his home and they went inside to bed.

Sunday morning Alice was up before David. After a trip to her bathroom, she crawled into Sir's bed and lay down beside him. As he was waking up, she saw his cock enlarge. That was her cue to begin her morning duty of sucking his cock until he came in her mouth. As soon as she put her mouth on him, he was fully awake and as she worked on his cock, he smoothed her hair back until he had her head held by two large handfuls of her lustrous locks. When he finally came Alice gladly sucked his cock for the last drops and then licked him clean.

"Good morning, Sir, did you sleep well?" Alice said as he released her hair.

David pulled her up until she was tucked under his arm. He kissed her and felt her wiggle against him. He knew she was wet, both from sucking his cock and his kissing her. He squeezed her breasts and rolled the nipples between his fingers. "You know, seeing Master Robert's girl last night, it gives me ideas about what I want to do with you," he joked. "What if I was to put a baby in you once a year? I could breed you and keep a baby at those breasts for at least ten or more years. What do you say to giving me ten children and letting me nurse from you to boot?"

Alice looked in his eyes and replied, "if you want to breed me, you will. I have given myself to you, although not formally, and if that is what you want, so be it. I know you will keep me safe and if you want ten children, I will happily carry them. I would also like to feed you from these breasts!"

He hugged her ever tighter. "I'm only joking, but I do want children in the future. It's just seeing Master Robert's girl, well she seemed so earthy and natural with her pregnant belly and big tits."

David slapped Alice playfully on the ass and told her he wanted coffee and something for breakfast. "We're going to the new house today and I want you to pack the picnic basket with the things I put in the fridge when I got home last night."

When breakfast finished and Alice had cleaned the kitchen, David told her what to wear. "I want you in a skirt and blouse. Put a pair of jeans in the car so you can change when we get to the job site. Remember, no panties or bra. Put the butt-plug in too. How are you doing with that anyway?"

Alice blushed, "I don't mind the butt-plug and I'm used to the restriction on the panties and bra. When will you give me a bigger one."

David put out his hands, had her turn around and 'bend and brace' so he could check the butt-plug. "Hm, it's not quite loose enough yet, I think in a few days we can go to the next larger size."

He turned it in her ass and elicited a moan from her. "You like that don't you? I look forward to using your ass the same way I use your pussy and mouth. I want all of you and that is part of it. A three-hole cum slut. My lady by day and whore by night and in the dungeon." He slapped her ass and told her to go and get ready to leave.

Smiling, Alice hurried to prepare for the trip to see the new house.

David had been driving for quite some time when Alice saw a familiar sign that said 'Clearwater'. She remembered it was where her father had bought a property some years back but she had sold it just before going with Evie to Paris and Florence. David had followed her and it was on the trip that he began to show her what her body could do with the right 'stimulation'. It was in Florence when she first began to acknowledge that she no longer held any animosity toward him and had in fact begun to love him.

The sound of the turn signal brought Alice back to the present. The newly rocked lane was not familiar but the mass of trees and undergrowth on both sides of it was. She sat forward in her seat and watched as the car would have passed into an open field of wildflowers that should have led to a lake. Part of the field was still there, but heavy equipment for moving earth and a partly finished building obscured the view of the lake.

"My god, what has happened to my dad's property?" Turning to David, "did you do this? How did you know this was part of my inheritance from my dad?" Tears streamed down her face as she looked back out of the window at the scars that had been made on the land.

David was shocked. "Your property! I bought this from a bank last May, just before you left for Europe with Evie." He tried to console Alice but she pulled away. "This was yours? I bought it from your dad's estate?"

Alice looked at David, "so it was you who bought it. Why didn't you tell me?"

"The bank was acting in the interests of an estate. The real estate agent I had didn't know whose estate and if they did, they didn't tell me." David was visibly upset. "I'm sorry if you don't like what you see here. I have an architect who has worked very hard to make this house eco-friendly and have as little adverse impact on the land as possible."

Finally, he seemed to be getting through to her. "When I was young, in high school, my Uncle Maurice would bring me and Auntie Lala here for picnics. He would tie her to that tree," he motioned to a smooth-bark tree surrounded by orange caution fencing, "and play with her. Before he died, he told me he had been trying to find out who owned the property so he could buy it but never did. He wanted me to buy it when I could and keep Lala's favorite tree."

"I'm sorry, I didn't know. Evie and I came out here once for a picnic, but that was the only time I'd seen it. This field," Alice gestured, "was full of beautiful wildflowers and the lake was so peaceful looking." She dried her eyes and blew her nose on a tissue. "I guess it was just the shock." She again looked out of the window. It was David's and she had put her trust in him so it was time to see his house.

She smiled at David and he told her he would get the picnic things while she changed into the jeans and walking shoes. He took her hand and led her to what was going to be the front door.

Walking into the house he could see that the finishing was not started. He'd been told the drywall was up in all of the rooms and the bathrooms had been tiled. Some of the bathroom fixtures were installed and the kitchen cabinets had been put in and were being protected by heavy paper covers. The floors were also covered so it was hard to tell what they were.

"This is the foyer," he began pointing to various rooms, "this is the dining room and here will be the kitchen, I wanted it all open so when you walk in the front you can see the lake and pool in the back." He turned and looked toward a large fireplace. "This is the family room area and," he took her hand and led her to another room, "this is more of a formal living room near the front door." They came to an opening which had been prepared for double doors. "Through here is the study/library and this is a door to the guest bathroom."

On the other side of the open great-room was another door opening which mirrored the one on the right side of the room where the study/library was located. "Through here is my own private space." He showed her a large bathroom, two big walk-in closets, and at the end of the short hall, "this is the master bedroom. It has a door to the outside, but these two walls are glass." He turned to the wall behind him, "The bed will fit here so the view to the lake will be the first thing I see when waking up."

They left the master suite and he pointed out two other doors in the great room which would also open onto the back. Next, he took her hand again and they went upstairs. A double door opening at the left of the stairs and he turned that way. "This is your suite." He led her into the bathroom and showed her the closet space. "You will also have a beautiful view of the lake and pool."

Alice stopped. David turned and started to take her hand. "Come, there is much more to see."

She was rooted to the spot. "My room? Why would I have a separate bedroom?"

David looked at her with a puzzled look on his face. "Alice, I have allowed you to sleep in my bed that one night, but that will not be the arrangement on a permanent basis. There will be no carpet in the bedrooms here, only tile or wood flooring and it would not make a great place to sleep. Unless you want to sleep on the floor at the foot of my bed like Auntie Lala did with my Uncle Maurice, you will want your own room."

She was stunned, "but why can't I sleep with you? We already have sex; you know me quite intimately. I don't understand."

David came back to her side. He took her hand and kissed it. "We have had sex and will continue to do so, but I will be your Dom and maybe someday your Master. Us sleeping together tends to blur the dynamic." Tenderly he moved an errant strand of hair and put it behind her ear. "Let me finish showing you what is on this floor and we can talk about sleeping arrangements in a setting more relaxed than a construction site."

He moved out of the suite and to the next room. "This will be the nursery," he pointed to seven more doors on the floor, "there are six more bedrooms and each has its own bath. The bedroom next to the nursery shares the bath through this door," he pointed to a door in the nursery. Next, he pointed to another door "this is the main bath for this floor and this," he opened a door near the landing of the stairs coming up from the main floor, "is the elevator which takes you up to the third floor."

David took a keychain from his trouser pocket. "This key operates the elevator." He motioned for Alice to get in with him and he turned the key in the panel in front of them and pushed the button below. The movement was smooth and the trip quick. "There is another exit from this room, but it is through here." David opened the door to a very spacious bathroom. The shower was huge and everything was in black. From the tiles on the floor and in the shower, some glossy and other matt, to the other fixtures and back-splash for the double-sinks, it was all black. She could see the mirrors were covered and the cabinet that took up almost one wall was also covered. There was also a bidet beside a regular toilet. The room had two doorways, one to a large closet and the other led to a set of stairs to the outside.

In the short hallway were two double doors which had already been installed. David opened them and soft lights came on. "This is the playroom." They both walked in. In the middle of the room sat a pile of cartons and what looked like furniture under some blue tarps. David pulled back a corner of the tarp to show her dark pieces of wood furniture and she recognized them immediately as item which would be found in a well-appointed dungeon.

The walls were red and the lighting was subdued. She realized that this vast room lay above 'her' suite on the second floor and above the master suite on the first floor. Anyone playing in this room would not disturb anyone in the rest of the house. As if David knew what she was thinking he said, "the floor and walls are soundproof so no amount of screaming will be heard beyond these walls." His hand swept the open room. "I know it looks big now, but it will not be so bare once the construction is done and the furniture and toys are moved in."

David pointed to the high ceiling and turned the lights up as he did, "these bolts will hold a lot of weight and I can put several restraint points, pulleys, or chains on them. I have a fellow member of our group who is a master rigger, rope-bondage." He caressed Alice's cheek, "I may have him do one of his intricate rope bindings on you one day; he could suspend you from the ceiling and let you see what it feels like to fly."

They went back through the doors, David closing them as they turned to the elevator. After their arrival on the second floor, David locked it. They went back to the first floor and into the formal living room space. He opened a door and showed Alice a large room with wires coming out of one wall. "This is the media room. There will be soundproofing installed on the walls for acoustic reasons, it will be great for movies or watching a game."

They went back into the kitchen where the picnic basket sat on a large island. David pulled a couple of boxes up to it, and Alice opened the hamper. David opened the fridge behind him and took out two bottles of water. Sitting on a box, Alice looked over at David and could see he seemed pleased with his house.

She took a large gulp of the water. "Sir, it's a wonderful looking house and it is situated on the property nicely. I like the windows here," she motioned to the ones which framed the lake and a swimming pool which was covered and protected from construction debris. "And the ones in the rooms on the second floor. I still don't understand the separate sleeping arrangements."

David put down his plastic fork, wiped his mouth on a paper napkin, and took Alice's hand. "What is our dynamic going to be? We aren't and never will be 'boyfriend/girlfriend.' I told you that was not how I will live my life. I tried vanilla and it was a disaster." He turned her hand over and looked at her palm. He raised it to his lips and kissed it, "you said you wanted to be my submissive. What have we been talking about and training you for all of these months?"

"For me to be your Dom and maybe in the future your Master, the power you give to me over you must and will always remain with me. To keep us focused on that we must not sleep together. If I allow you to sleep in my bed on occasion, or more likely on the floor at the foot of my bed, it will be because of a special circumstance. I will be the one to determine that, not you. You can give me your opinion, but I'll not have you nagging me about it."

"Look Alice," he picked up her other hand, all effort to eat their picnic forgotten. "When and if I accept you as my sub, when I collar you in a public ceremony in front of the other Doms and Masters in our group, we will be married. Now I know that married couples sleep together and that is why, on our wedding night, I will most joyously have you sleep beside me." He could tell his words were affecting the wetness of her pussy. "We will be married in front of family and friends in a pure vanilla ceremony. However, the next night, I will do like my uncle did and have your formal collaring ceremony. You will be my sub, my most beautiful and obedient sub, for all of the people in our M/s, D/s community to applaud for joining in a formal arrangement. From that time forward, while we will have plenty of sex, we will not spend the night in the same bed."

There it was, the answer to a question that had been nagging Alice since she had moved into the house with the dungeon where Lala had been the slave of David's uncle. Why did Lala have her own room separate from her Master and why was it so momentous that at his last, he had allowed his slave to lie in the bed next to him while she held him as he breathed his last? Here was the answer. It had never occurred to her but it was sitting right in front of her.

"I, uh, I'd never thought about that. I'm uh, this is pretty important. I wish you had said something about the sleeping arrangements before," Alice pulled her hands away and put them in her lap, "I need to think about this." She stood up and started to clear the things away.

David stood next to her and took the carton of potato salad out of her hand, "Alice, it says nothing about not sleeping with you because I don't love you, it's about the power in the relationship. That you will give, freely, to me and it will be my job to keep you safe, loved, and help you reach your full potential as a woman of great promise." He reached into his pocket, pulled out a box, and opened. "Alice, this house will be finished in about six months. I want to marry you when it is ready for us to move in and have our wedding night in that master bedroom over there." He took the ring from the box and took her hand, before slipping it on her left ring finger, "Please say you will marry me. Be my wife, be my most treasured love."

Alice hesitated. After everything he had told her today, did she want to live her life sleeping in an empty bed? He said he wanted children, the way he had the rooms arranged it would be she having the children and caring for them while he slept the night away in his own big suite, absent when a night feeding or a sick baby needed both of its parents. Then she remembered the long talks, the training he'd already had been doing with her to turn her into a sub. She wanted to be his sub, in fact she was finding out that deep inside of her she needed to be his sub and that without him, she would feel terribly empty and on some even deeper level, craved the pain/pleasure the lifestyle promised. She looked in his eyes and gave the only answer she could, "Yes, yes I'll marry you."

David slipped the ring on her finger and pulled her into his arms.

ENGAGEMENT!

D avid parted Alice's lips in a deep kiss that seemed to last forever. Their tongues battled, his mastering hers and she relenting and allowing him full access. She was breathless when he finally let her up. He had French-kissed her before, but never in this way. Alice worried that the flood of juices it had release into her sex would spill over and wet her jeans.

David unbuttoned the pants she was wearing and slipped them down. Off came the heavy shoes she had been told to wear and the jeans. He lifted her onto the kitchen island. He pushed her legs apart and placed her feet on the edge before pulling her ass to the edge. Opening his pants, he pulled his fully erect cock from his pants and put it up against her clit.

The up and down movement over her sex was driving her wild. He took both of her hands in one of his and with the other, guided himself into her pussy. Slowly at first, he penetrated her with the head of his cock and then, pulling it out, used it to tap her clit. Finally, he put it in her all the way to the balls and began to fuck her.

With his now free hand he pushed her blouse up above her breasts. The nipples were hard and the pert breasts were tempting him to suck them. He pulled and rolled the nipples as he continued a slow rhythm of the in and out of his cock.

"Hands above your head," David ordered in a deep, throaty voice. He released her hands and she complied to his command. With his free thumb he circled his girl's clit with it and then began to stimulate it more quickly as his rhythmic fucking grew faster and harder. He could tell she was on the edge. "You will not come unless I give you permission!"

"Yes, sir, but may I come, please!" Alice begged. The stimulation he was giving her had her so close to the edge then he pulled his hand from their nipple play and slowed his thrusting cock and the thumb which was working on her pulsing clit. "Oh, Sir, please, please" she cried.

"Are you a good girl?" he asked in a growl.

"Yes, Sir," she breathed.

"And who gets to come?" he growled in reply.

"Only good girls, Sir?" she whispered shakily.

He began to speed up and resumed his thumb play of her clit. David pounded into her and now had her back to the edge. "Then come my good girl, come!" he shouted.

Alice arched her back and exploded in an orgasm that even surprised David. Her muscles of her passage tightened around his cock in a way it hadn't before and it drove him on and on. The continued stimulation of her clit with his thumb and now fingers kept the orgasms rolling through her. David reached his peak and caught her last orgasm with his. As he continued to pump his seed into her, he gave her one last orgasm with his hand on her clit. Then both of them stilled and held their positions until he began to slide out of her.

Reaching over to the picnic basket he rummaged around and pulled out some napkins and individually wrapped wet wipes. He tore open a wet wipe and with a napkin under his cock, slowly removed it and began cleaning up himself and as the cum began to ooze out of Alice's pussy he caught it in the napkin and cleaned her.

Alice still lay on the island. He pulled his pants up and reaching for Alice's, he began to put her legs into hers. She was told to "sit," and with both hands he took her by the waist and set her on the floor. He pulled up her pants and then helped her back into her footwear.

She slumped against him and her righted her. Looking into her eyes he could see she was still not fully in the now. He held her against him and supported her until she had roused enough to stand on her own. Her tousled hair and the flush on her face told him that this was one trip to the house they both would never forget.

Quickly he packed the things away in the picnic basket and took another two bottles of water from the fridge. He put the things in the car and helped Alice into her seat. He pulled her blouse closed and buttoned it. Yes, he would have to think more about those breasts.

Alice sat on the floor at the foot of her Sir's bed in the master bedroom. He was in the shower. The trip to the new house had been exciting and had opened new sensations in the sex she had experienced with her soon to be Dom. He had given her an engagement ring, she had accepted his proposal of marriage, and the celebratory sex on the island in the unfinished kitchen had been more than she could have ever imagined.

After David put her in the car for the ride back to the house, it took Alice almost forty-five minutes to fully recover enough for a meaningful conversation between the two. David did call his parents and asked if they would be at home in the evening and what time would be good for him to come by. He was bringing a friend with him. David's father answered the phone and told him eight would be good.

Alice heard David get out of the shower and expected him to be out of the bathroom very soon. He'd told Alice about the visit they would make to his parent's house that evening and she was to prepare herself. Her hair was still damp from her shower, but she wanted to know what her Sir wanted her to wear before she finished doing all of her preparations.

Alice had met his parent's when she had noticed his mother choaking on something in a restaurant while she and Evie had been on one of their mini vacations on a school break. Alice's quick action got the mother onto the floor, the fish bone extracted from her throat, and Alice beginning CPR before the EMS could arrive. She hadn't known David, except for a cryptic warning from her old family doctor, and it had tainted her opinion of David until he had finally shown her that his side of the story was much different than what the family doctor had led her to believe. Now, she was going to meet the parents as David's fiancé.

Alice shifted into a kneeling position with her head bowed. The movement caught David's eye and it surprised him that his girl was in his room and not in hers getting ready for the evening. They would be going out to dinner first and he wanted plenty of time to eat before the appointment with his parents at eight o'clock.

"Alice," David said, "why aren't you ready? We don't have much time and I don't want to rush through our meal." A closer look at his girl and he could see she had showered because her hair was still damp. "Go dry your hair and dress."

"Please, Sir, I don't know what you want me to wear and it will depend on the outfit as to how I shall fix my hair. Can you choose or give me directions in this?" Her head was still bowed, with her hands palms up and resting on her thighs, she couldn't even see the engagement ring David had put on her just that afternoon. This visit to his parents was important and she wanted everything to be right.

"Very well, put the dark blue silk on, wear stockings and a garter belt, the dress has a built-in bra, and of course, no panties. Black stockings, the ones I got you with the seam up the back." He paused at the closet door, "oh, and the shoes that are in the box in your closet." He dismissed her and told her she had fifteen minutes to meet him downstairs.

Hair dried and put in a soft French braid, the lightest of make-up with glossy lips, and dressed as her Sir directed, Alice stood waiting for David when he came out of the dungeon. Alice raised her dress and slipped to her stockinged knees in a formal kneel. Head bowed she waited until he spoke to her.

"Alice you are beautiful tonight but please stand so we can leave." He said with a note of exasperation in his voice.

She rose to her feet and steadied herself on the strappy heels with the red soles he had bought her. An extravagant gift which she would thank him for after her first order of business was addressed. "Permission to speak, Sir," she said strongly.

"Alice, we have to go and of course you can speak, you're not on any speech restriction tonight, at least not yet. Say what you want." His exasperation was growing and it showed in his voice.

"Sir, you have asked me to marry you and I've accepted, gladly I want to add." Alice smiled as she looked at her Sir. "Now, you want to tell your parents, but before you do, I want you to know, well," she hesitated before going on, "well, it's customary for the bride's family to pay for the wedding but since my parents, in fact my whole family is dead, I will pay for it." There she'd said it. He had to know she would do what was expected.

David voice softened, "nonsense, I will pay for it. As you said, you have no family and except for a few friends you have, all or most of the guests will be my family, friends, and collogues. I know your aunt and family left you some money, but that is for you." He put his hand in the small of her back to guide her forward but she didn't budge.

"David, my family specifically left money to pay for my wedding. My father made the provision in his will and my mother affirmed it in hers'." She looked at him for understanding.

David dropped his hand, "are you defying me? I told you I would pay for it, you can use your money for your dress and things, but the wedding is on me. Now remember who you are before I make it clearer to you."

Alice didn't move. She needed him to know he was not getting a pauper or a girl looking for any money he may have, but someone who, if needed, could live quite well without him, at least financially. He had to know this.

David stepped back and looked in Alice's eyes. She was in open defiance and he would not have that. "Present and show me!" The words were like a slap on Alice's face. She pulled her dress up and tucked it into the band of her garter belt. She stood in front of David with her feet as far apart as she could put them without falling over and her pelvis thrust forward. With both hands she pulled back her labia, exposing her clit and opening to her pussy. "Who does that belong to, who have you pledged it to?" David said sharply.

Alice bowed her head in surrender, "You Sir, only you."

With a slap of his open hand, he struck her sex. "Remember that. Now arrange yourself to leave, you've made us late." Alice smoothed her dress and picked up her evening bag from the front table. David helped her on with her Kami Worth jacket and guided her out of the door. Whispering in her ear, "I will use you tonight, you will not defy me and your punishment will be two-fold. Now vanilla-up for my parents."

The restaurant David had chosen was near the theatre where Hamlet was being performed by a touring company from Britain. The clientele was usually those people who either ate before the show or after. Since the play was ongoing, this was the best time to get a good table. David chose sea bass for them both without any wine. He knew there would be toasts to his engagement later and didn't wish to drive impaired.

It was a short drive up the hill to his parent's home. He had never taken Alice here, in fact, he'd not taken a girl to his parent's house since the high school prom. He'd taken one of his cousins so that didn't count. Through the gates and down the drive, he could see lights on in the formal living room and an extra car parked in front of the house.

David was not impressed with this house. It was where he grew up and except for a couple of summers during his undergraduate years, he hadn't lived in it since graduating from high school. He didn't visit very often but mostly saw his parents at one of the restaurants his father owned or at a coffee shop in one or other of the office buildings in his portfolio.

The door opened as they approached and David guided Alice inside to a substantial foyer. It soared three stories and with a skylight of multicolored mosaic glass, the effect when the sun hit would be to bath the white marble floor in rainbow hues. White marble pillars supported the massive room. Cora and Alexander Khoury stood at the entrance of an equally massive room to their right. The double doorway framed them both perfectly.

Taking Alice's hand David led her to them. "Mother, Father, I think you remember Miss Blake, uh Alice Blake. She is the one who saved your life that time." David's face wore a big smile while Alice also smiled, but hers' was more reserved. Alice extended her hand, first to Cora Khoury and then to David's father, Alexander.

"Of course, I remember her, how could I forget." Cora shook the proffered hand and continued. "Welcome to our home." Looking over at David, "our son should have brought you here sooner so I could thank you personally."

Alexander took Alice's hand and led her into the formal living room. Alice looked around and saw traditional furniture, many of them antiques, but with sophisticated hues and textures. David took Alice's hand from his father and sat Alice on a cream-colored sofa and eased in beside her.

"I had the pleasure of seeing Miss Blake, uh, Alice one night at my restaurant. I think you were there with the Rossi boy, a grandson of Gino if I'm not mistaken." Turning to Alice, "how is he by the way."

Alice looked at David, "I wouldn't know sir, I am no longer seeing him, for almost a year now."

"Father, mother," David said. He stood for more emphasis, "I asked to visit tonight because I've asked Alice to marry me and," he reached down and pulled her to her feet, "she has accepted. We'll be married in about six months." He knew it might be a surprise to his parents but the shock on their faces he wasn't prepared for at all.

His mother was the first on her feet. "I'm surprised son, uh, we know nothing about her and for me to put together a wedding for you in less than six months, you have to push that back, a year or more would give me enough time." Distressed, she turned away from him.

"Son," Alex said, looking at Alice, "we are grateful for her, you know, for your mother and all, but surely there is some other compensation she would prefer. Have you thought about this?" His stare bored into David. "Think about the stress this will put on your mother. Slow down son, you don't need this right now."

David looked from one parent to the other. A slight tug on his hand brought his gaze to Alice. Her eyes glistened and he knew this rejection was all too evident to her. He put his arm around her shoulders. She whispered in his ear, "Bathroom, I want the bathroom."

Pointing her in the right direction she made her excuses and left the room to find some safety in a restroom. It was large with a separate closet for the toilet and an antique dresser which had been modified to hold the two porcelain vessels that served as sinks. A gold framed mirror and hardware shone against the earthy dark green on the walls. A small upholstered chair sat in a corner and a stack of fluffy towels were laid out for guests to use.

Alice was stunned. She had never been treated, dismissed, spoken about as if she wasn't even in the room, like this before. She examined her visage in the mirror and didn't find it wanting. She was dressed smartly but not overly conservative but as one of her age would dress when going to a dinner or on a visit. She washed her hands and used a soft towel. Hm, even the towels were scented.

She rallied and prepared to return to the living room. Raised voices could be heard but they were not speaking English but French. Of course, David's mother was raised in Beirut and her first language was French as it was with most of the upper-class Christian women. Alice stopped to listen when she heard her name.

"David, we don't know anything about her." His mother's voice softened a little. "I have tried to introduce you to more than a dozen suitable girls, girls from outstanding families. Virgins who would give you sons and daughters. You've never shown interest but then you come with this girl?" Cora Khoury's voice rose an octave "What's her background? Where did she go to school? Her parents, who are her parents."

David shot back, "her parents are both dead, in fact all of her relatives are dead. She is from Oakland and until her mother passed away, they had a home as outstanding, if not more so, than the one we are in now. She is independently wealthy in her own right and manages her own portfolio from an office in downtown."

Alex intervened, "why the rush son? She can't be pregnant or you would want to marry quickly. Why not wait and let me have her checked out. Your cousin George can do that, he has contacts in the police."

Alice was shocked. Sometimes she wished she didn't know French. Squaring her shoulders, she went back into the room where David's parents were tearing apart her life and character. "Such a pretty guest bathroom!" she had directed her comments to Cora, "the rest of your home must be equally as lovely. Your home is almost as big as the one where I grew up. Oh, it was my grandfather's house, but we had all lived there with him." She paused for a moment for dramatic flair, "it was listed on the National Register and is now the Howard Blake Museum, named after great grand-dad."

Everyone in this part of the United States knew who Howard Blake was and the inventions he was responsible for in medical devices and equipment. Not a surgeon in the world didn't have a set of Blake retractors or at least wished they had them when doing delicate surgeries. The Blake filter, used to prevent blood clots from going into a patient's heart, lungs, or brain, had been used for more than forty years and installed correctly, had a superior success rate.

All three of the Khoury clan were stunned. David had never associated Alice's last name to the famous family and his parents were equally silenced. Alice continued, "as for the wedding, my father specifically set aside close to one hundred thousand dollars in his will for my wedding when I was twelve and with the time, interest, and compounding, well, it is more than enough to pay for whatever I choose." Looking straight at David's mother, "it is the bride's place to pay for the wedding she wants, and I've already told David that is what I will do." Turning to the father, "and you will be happy to know that, if we get married, I'll not embarrass David by asking him to sign a pre-nuptial agreement to protect the rest of my estate, even though the family attorney has told me in the strongest terms that I should."

No one made a sound. She turned to David and put her hand on his arm and softly said. "I would like to go home now, please." She turned and started for the door, then she stopped. Turning back toward the people in the room, "if you are worried about my virginity, David took it." She stuck a thoughtful pose, "and I really must write to my French governess, she taught me the most perfect and beautiful Parisian French." Alice turned and made for the front door.

David caught up in time to help her into her jacket. The silence in the room behind her was broken by a mixture of French and another language, probably Lebanese Arabic. Silently David and Alice walked to the car and drove to Uncle Maurice's old house. Not a word was said.

At the front door, David unlocked it and Alice followed him in and made a beeline to the stairs. "Stop" David commanded. "You will come back here and ask permission to leave the room." Alice turned and approached David. "On your knees, I haven't dismissed you and there is some punishment due you tonight."

Alice placed her purse on the hall table and pulled up her dress to sink to her knees, the fabric of the dress pooling around her. Her head was bowed and her hands were open, palms up, resting on her thighs in a formal kneel. "Open your legs more. You need to learn this correctly if you are to become a good sub."

A tear fell on the dark blue silk of Alice's dress. Her head shot up and her tear-glistened eyes fixed on David. "Perhaps I'm not the sub for you if you didn't even take time to find out anything about me. I've held nothing back from you and if you had asked me, I would have told you. To be humiliated like that, no, no this is wrong." Alice stood and grabbed her purse. The keys to the Shelby were in there as well as her credit cards. She snatched her jacket and ran out of the door.

She got the door to the car open and was pulling out of the drive when David came and knocked on her door. "Come back in here. Where do you think you are going at this hour of the night?" The car continued to roll down the drive and she sped off toward town.

The light drizzle which had started as they were driving from his parent's house turned into a downpour. David stood watching the taillights of the Shelby disappear into the night. He was soaked by the rain but didn't feel a drop, his life, his dreams, lay shattered at his feet. A ringing of the phone in his pocket finally brought him around and he hurried back into the house. It must be Alice calling him, but it was his father's number showing on the caller ID.

He answered. "We are so sorry for this evening son, bring her back here so we can apologize." He could hear the distress in his father's voice and he thought he could hear his mother crying. "Neither of us had any idea of who she was, why didn't you tell us, let us get to know her before springing this on us?"

David let out a long sigh, "it's over dad, she's gone, tell mother 'Thank you' for destroying my life. She was my one and now I don't know how I'll ever get a chance to talk to her, much less get her back." He dropped the call. He didn't want to talk to them tonight.

Alice stopped at a light and decided to pull over to call about a room. She rummaged around for her phone and found it at the bottom of her bag. She missed her laptop but looked up the Excelsior Hotel and called them. "Why yes miss Blake, we have a small suite. Will that be for one night? And for one person?" she heard the clacking of the keys on a keyboard, "Excellent, we'll be expecting you."

Before going to the hotel, she decided to stop at one of the storage units she had rented on a yearly basis for the things that had come from her family home and the aunt's cottage. She punched in the number of the outer gate and Uncle Buddy's Storage lay before her. The climate-controlled unit she wanted was in the third building on the right. She had put digital locks on all of her units and had memorized the codes long ago.

The door swung open and she flipped the light switch. She could see what she wanted was right where she remembered it. A small Louis Vuitton case and travel bag were on a dresser where she still had a selection of underthings, jeans, and tops. She took what she needed and would stop to pick up some toiletries on the way to the hotel. A box near the dresser had some shoes in it and she choose some house shoes and a pair of pumps to wear outside.

Back on the street, she turned into a 24-hour pharmacy and went in to buy what she needed. A swipe of her card and only one more stop was necessary. She turned on Carlyle Street and went two blocks down to a building which sat in the middle of one block.

Porter's Antiques was dark as was the apartment above it. Driving around the block, Alice looked to see if the owner's car was parked anywhere. Nothing.

Alice went back to the main road she had been on and drove for several minutes and parked under the portico of the Excelsior. A boutique hotel and little known to the general public, the Excelsior catered to a select clientele. Alice's mother had loved coming her when they had to be in town for anything from shopping and later, for cancer treatments. Sometimes the drive back to Oakland was just more than her mother could stand. Alice would sit in the back of the limo with her mother wrapped in a blanket weak but begging to stop so she could rest. Henry, well Albert Henry, her mother's driver would help her get her mother into a room and then wait until she was strong enough to go on, even if it was all night.

The porter took out her luggage and she gave her key to the valet. The assistant manager stood in the foyer and offered pleas-antries but Alice just told her she wanted to go to her suite. After walking down a long hallway, the middle-aged lady put her keycard in the door and waited for Alice to enter. The bags were brought in and the door closed behind them. Alice got out her house shoes and kicked off the shoes David had ordered her to wear. After hanging up her dress and jacket, removing her garter belt and stockings, she put on one of the plush robes from the bathroom.

Alice curled up on the bed and wept. In her purse, her silenced phone vibrated as David tried to call. As light began to peek into the room from the window, Alice, cried out, and dried out, finally fell into a troubled sleep. Not for the first time in her life had she lost everything that meant anything to her, but for her this was the most tragic loss of all.

Alice roused from her sleep about ten and called down to the desk. She added another two nights to her stay and was acknowl-edged with a cheery "No problem." Getting up to use the bathroom she looked at herself in the mirror, sipped some water, and returned to bed. Finally at close to two she got up, showered, and put some jeans and a top on.

Her cell phone was in her purse and she saw several voicemails, texts, and emails from David. Great, was she again going to be the subject of his stalking? She should have listened to Salek. The last text was from Evie, she checked the time and it was still early enough for her to call.

Evie answered on the first ring. "What in the hell is going on over there? David is burning up the phone lines and trying to destroy the internet trying to find you? Where are you?"

"Well, hello to you, too." Alice said calmly. "I'm in Green Valley and I don't want to talk to David."

"Alice, what happened? He told me he asked you to marry him, even gave you an engagement ring but when he took you to meet the parents they freaked and when he took you home you bolted. God girl, what is going on?" Evie was worried and Alice wished David hadn't involved her in this.

"Yes, that is about right. They all but called me a gold-digging slut who was after David for his money. I didn't know he has any besides his medical salary. Anyway, they yelled at each other in French when I was out of the room but I understood it all. God, I've never been so humiliated in all of my life. When we got home, well, let's just say things went from bad to very much worse. I told him it was over, took my car, and left. That's it."

"Alice, David has been on the phone with me for hours and my God girl, the guy really loves you. He says you are the only one for him and that he feels like his whole world has been shattered. At least talk to him or let me call him and let him know you are okay." Evie wanted to be the peacemaker.

She thought for several seconds, "okay Evie, you can call him and tell him I'm okay. I'll have someone come and get my clothes and other things in the next few days. I'll send him his ring back via courier. His parents should be happy, now he can go marry some virginal girl his mother picks out for him." Before she hung up Evie asked her where she was. "If I don't tell you then you won't be lying to him when you tell him you don't know. Bye my friend." Alice hung up the call.

Alice took the elevator down and walked out of the hotel. There was a café on the corner that she knew had good coffee and fresh pastries. She took a seat in the window and looked out onto the street. For a Monday the traffic and people going to and from their work was about normal for this part of town. Two cups of coffee and a roll later she was ready to return to her room. As she passed the front desk, she took a copy of the financial paper they had free for their guests.

In the room, a yellow pages directory gave her the name of a reputable courier firm and on another page the number of Porter's Antiques. Jesse Porter had been a friend of Alice's mom and she knew Alice quiet well. Depending upon what happened in the next few days, she would ask Jesse Porter to get her things from the house where she had been living. First though, she called the courier.

Twenty minutes later the boy from the courier firm had picked up the envelope with David's ring in it and put it in one of their padded pouches. After signing and making it clear that Dr. Khoury was not to know where the package had originated from, no matter how much of a bribe he might offer, she handed over the ring and closed the door.

It was late in Florence but Evie was back on the phone. "Alice, think about what you are doing. He loves you; he came all the way to Europe to make sure you were okay and take you home. At least talk to him, give him a chance. The two of you together, you were perfect."

"Evie, there is a lot more to it than you know but it's something that is just between David and I. I'll find a place to live tomorrow and let you know how I'm doing. Sleep now. I'll land on my feet; I just have to get used to the idea I'll have to do it on my own." She terminated the call.

Forty-five minutes later the house phone rang and an operator was whispering to her that there was a man at the front desk looking for her. It was the house line. "Thank you for letting me know." Alice hung up.

Within seconds there was a knock on her door. Well, it was going to have to happen sometime, best to get it over. She closed the door to the bedroom and opened the door. Alice was surprised to find Alex and Cora Khoury standing in the doorway. David was not in sight.

Cora Khoury stepped forward. "Might we come in, please?"

Alice thought about it and stepped back to allow them in. David's parents sat together on the sofa while she faced them in one of the wing-backed chairs. Alice had offered to get room service to bring them something but they declined.

"Miss Blake, Alice," Cora Khoury started, "I am profoundly and deeply sorry for what happened at our home. It's just, as a mother, I spend my time worrying over my only child. When one day you have children, you will begin to understand this. David has never brought a girl home nor really showed much interest in any of the girls, uh, women we have introduced him to. He just wasn't interested." She looked around at her husband with pleading eyes.

Alexander Khoury cleared his throat. "I would like to explain some things to you and hopefully you will understand our concern better. Cora, uh my wife's grandmother, was an only child as was her mother. Cora's great-grandfather had a vast business but he was old fashioned and wrote in his will that only a male of his direct line could inherit his estate. David is the first male heir in the direct line." Cora patted his arm in support, "David will inherit this when he marries." Alex pulled a handkerchief out of his breast pocket and gave it to his wife.

Alice looked between the two. "I didn't know. David and I never talked about money or inheritances." She stood up and got a glass of water for Mrs. Khoury from the bar at the end of the sitting room. "I was actually surprised that David hadn't looked into my life closer. I thought he knew about my family, who I came from, and the extent of the portfolio I manage."

Alex rose to face her but Cora stood and put her hand on his arm. She said, "Alice, our son is devastated. I, we, can see just how much he loves you. Won't you go back to him? Ease his pain, I'm his mother, don't make my child suffer because of our mistakes about you. Please?" Close to tears her husband hugged her to him.

Alex comforted his wife as she sobbed quietly. "Alice," Alice put her hand up to stop him.

"I wish I could help, but it's complicated. David has to ask me to come back to him, but not before he can understand the hurt and damage he has done to us and to me personally. It's up to him now. I'm sure you will tell him where I am, but only he knows what is at stake and what it takes to fix this." Alice showed them to the door and promised she would take David's next phone call.

It didn't take long. Within ten minutes David's call came through. Quietly and with a voice strained with emotion he asked if he could see her. She relented and told him he could come to the hotel.

Before David arrived a large bouquet of roses was delivered to her room. Next, the room service waiter rolled in a cart with two plates covered with sterling silver cloches proudly bearing the crest of the hotel and a bottle of champagne chilling in a sterling silver ice bucket. David arrived soon after.

Alice opened the door and stepped back so he could enter. There was no touching, no hello kiss, simply a respect for each other's boundaries. "Come sit," Alice said motioning to the table with the dinner service spread on it, "whatever you've ordered will get cold."

"Alice, uh, okay, thank you." He held her chair and then sat opposite her. The meal was a veal cutlet, vegetables, and a small salad. "If you want dessert, just tell me and I'll call it in."

"David, relax, this is just fine. I don't have much of an appetite." Alice dabbed at her mouth with her napkin and laid it down beside a mostly full plate. "I don't really want anything to eat, thank you."

"You need …," David began and then thought better of it. "I'm sorry."

Alice sighed, "David, you came here to talk, at least I thought that is what you wanted to do, so why don't you start. Let's see how this goes." Alice pushed her chair back and removing her dishes to the food cart, sat back down at her empty place.

David took his things away also and resumed his seat. "Alice, I just don't know what to say, I had no idea what your family's background was. I saw the little cottage your aunt lived in and you had mentioned you had gone to live with her after your mother passed and the family home was sold."

"Aunt Dorie was my mother's aunt on her mother's side. She lived in the cottage because that is where she waited for her husband to come home from the Korean War. He never did and she stayed where she was. She could have lived anywhere, but she wouldn't budge." Alice told him. "Your parents have already been here and given me their deep and sincere apologies, I need to hear what you have to say about you, us, and if there still is an us."

David cleared his throat. "Alice there will always be an us. You don't get it do you?" He looked at her and shook his head, "I was never going to fall in love, that was for vanilla people and I had known for years I was anything but vanilla but then you came along. You saved my mom's life and stole my heart all at the same time and never realized what you had done." He found a crumb on the table in front of him and pushed it around with one of his long index fingers. "When you drove away, when those taillights disappeared into the night, you pulled my heart out of my chest and drug it down the street behind you."

Alice looked deep into his eyes, "then you really want me?" she said, barely above a whisper.

David ran both hands through his hair, "want you, want you, I need you more than anything and uh, please come home." He reached out for her hand but she pulled it back.

"Uh, before, we can go forward, we still have something to discuss," started Alice, "one of the things you told me when you were telling me about the Dom/sub dynamic was that if I ever wanted out, that was it, no second chances, and I should never expect you to come after me. Doesn't that still apply?"

David put his head in his hands and shook it from side to side. "Little Alice, I have not accepted you yet, that doesn't apply to this, at least not wholly. I am upset that you broke protocol when you dashed out of the house and didn't obey me when I told you to stop." He looked at her, "I don't know how many things you have earned a punishment for, but there were extenuating circumstances so I'll take that into account." He waited for her to continue.

"Then I guess," Alice said, "there is just the question of a wedding" David put his hand up to signal her to stop.

"We have to talk about a wedding. I don't see your engagement ring. How can we talk wedding without that?" His eyes had some of the old mischief in them. He reached into his breast pocket. "Is this the one you are missing?" David reached across the table and put the ring in front of Alice. "I have talked with my parents and they think you should plan and pay for the wedding you want. And I, well, I know how much it means to you, so I agree also."

Alice picked up the ring and put it on her finger. She looked down at it and tears welled up in her eyes. One slipped out and fell on the table in front of them. David reached over and handed her a handkerchief. "Why is it women never have one when they need it?"

Alice looked at him, "why do men keep making it necessary for a woman to need one?"

WE'RE ALL GOOD

The bottle of champagne sat in the water from the melted ice. Both had reached room temperature. On the sofa, David sat with a sleeping Alice in his lap. There had been a lot of kissing and fondling, but no sex. He knew, well they both understood, there were issues which still needed to be worked through before they could go forward.

Between the kissing and moments of silence in each other's arms, they had talked. David had other subs before Alice, but none had come to him who were not at least partially trained and the break that had happened two nights' before was normal for people new to the lifestyle. It had never happened to him personally but he had known about it from others. What would happen in the next few days would determine how the life he wanted with Alice would go forward. He knew someone who could help but only if Alice was open to the help.

Doctor Johnathan Morris, also known as Master Morris, was a retired psychiatrist and kink-friendly doctor. He was known as Jon to his friends and David had known him for years. As an old friend of his Uncle Maurice, he was once an active member of the circle of Masters and Dominants who made up the bulk of David's friends in the kink community. He was no longer as active, but his mind was still as sharp as ever.

David was not ashamed that he had, on occasion, consulted Jon on a professional basis and not always about his kinky side but on other, private matters as well. When he'd thought everything was lost with Alice because of how his parents had treated her, the idea of asking for Jon's help wasn't far below the surface. After what he and Alice had discussed last night, he knew Master Morris could help them both. Alice shifted slightly in his lap and a look at his wristwatch told him it would be another hour before Jon would be up. He also wanted to broach the subject with Alice about doing a consult with the good doctor.

He smoothed a strand of hair away from Alice's face as he looked down on his girl. His girl. Cute and innocent, super smart, loveable, adorable, exasperating, frustrating, gorgeous, sometimes obedient but at others disruptive, his girl. He loved her, oh God how he loved her and depending upon how the next few days would unfold, he just might have to give her up, a fate he didn't want but dreaded to contemplate.

Alice again stirred in his lap and as she opened her eyes the look in them reflected his love. "Good morning little one." David said, brushing her mouth with his lips. "Are you ready for some coffee and breakfast, you hardly ate last night. You need to look after yourself better." Her smile lit up her face as she nodded and slipped off of his lap for a trip to the bathroom.

While she was gone David called for room service and got them both a bottle of water from the fridge at the wet bar. He took the bottle of champagne and put it on its side in the fridge, they may want it later. Alice returned from the bathroom and David took his turn.

While David was in the bathroom Alice came in to take a shower. He watched her in the mirror as he shaved. Her lean, toned body, generous breasts, and her long shapely legs. Oh, how he wanted to join her, help her wash, and dry her body when she got out, water dripping from her nipples and sheening down her body. It was all he could do to keep from fucking her right there, up against the bathroom sink.

David was still in the shower when the breakfast arrived and Alice signed for the food and went into the bathroom to tell him the food was there. It was her turn to look at David as he finished his morning routine. His naked body, a slight olive tint to his skin, a testament to his exotic Lebanese heritage, looked like the statue of David by Michelangelo which was in the Pitti Palace Museum. Toned and muscles taught from working out in the hospital gym, he was a sight to behold. Strong arms, long muscular legs, and abbs you could scrub clothes on. His cock, lying among a mass of well-groomed pubic hair, hung low even when not aroused and his ball sack was appropriately proportioned. The sight of him made Alice wet and it was all she could do to stop herself from taking his cock in her mouth and drinking of his cum.

Shaking her head, she remembered why she had come into the bathroom and informed David that the breakfast would soon be cold. Turning to leave, he stepped forward and took her hand. "Alice, you don't know how much I've missed you," he sighed, "we have to make this right, you know that, don't you?" Alice nodded as she went to pour the coffee.

David sat down across from Alice and sipped his morning coffee. "Alice, I feel like we still have some issues we need to address. And, I want us to see someone who might be able to help."

She set down her cup and looked into his eyes. She thought a moment and nodded, "yes, I think you may be right, but who, do you know someone? I mean someone who knows about what our dynamic or what it should be?"

David smiled. "Yes, and you have met him already." When he saw the puzzled look on her face he went on, "the other night, Master Morris. In reality he is Dr. Johnathan Morris, he's retired from his practice, but I've consulted with him before and he's good, really good at what he does. I guess being in the lifestyle himself makes it easier to understand some of the problems that can come up. He is also an old friend of my Uncle Maurice."

"I'll can call him and find out when we can see him. That is if you like." Now the ball was in Alice's court. Did she really want this relationship to go forward or not?

Alice's eyes brightened and she smiled at David, "of course I would like. Would it be us together, just me, what?" She asked.

"Let's let Jon make that decision after he talks to us. I'll call him and see if he can see us today." David selected Morris' name from his contacts and put the phone to his ear. He was told that he could see them in about a half hour. David thanked him and hung up. Turning to Alice, he told her they needed to eat up because Jon did not like people being late.

Jon Morris stood in his open door waiting for David and Alice to walk up the stairs, "Good morning you two! Isn't it a lovely day! Come in, come in." His enthusiasm was infectious and both Alice and David smiled broadly as he bid them to have a seat in his old office. A pot of coffee and three mugs sat on a table between them. Alice and David were on a comfy couch and Jon sat in a wing-backed chair across from them.

After pleasantries were exchanged and Jon had poured them each a coffee, he began by asking David what had brought them here. He assured them that anything that was said would be held in the strictest confidence. "I may be retired but I haven't lost my ethical standards."

David began by talking about what had happened on Sunday, the visit to the new house, him asking Alice to marry him and her accepting, but also about the disastrous visit to his parents. "When we got home I had her kneel. She snapped, grabbed her purse, took her car and left, but not before telling me it was over. She had a courier bring the engagement ring back on Monday." David looked over to Alice and saw her eyes glisten with tears yet to be shed.

"Hmm," Jon said as he watched the body language of the two. "Is that about how you remember it Alice? Anything you would like to add?"

Alice was holding David's hand and she gave it a squeeze. "Yes, except he left out the incredible sex we had after he asked me to marry him and then again when we got home from seeing the house. He's pretty well covered it." She shifted a bit in her seat and both men understood her thoughts and memories were arousing her. She continued, "David had told me once, at almost the beginning of our relationship when he explained his lifestyle and vision, that this was a one-shot deal. If I ever wanted out, well, there would be no second chance and he wouldn't chase after me. It had to be all the way with his vision without compromise." She took a sip of her coffee before continuing, "when I told him I was finished and ran out of the house I was afraid he wouldn't want me back. I was terrified and although I can take care of myself, not being a part of him left me devastated, rudderless, and quite frankly, without him I'd be a mess."

Before anyone could answer to what she'd said, she continued, "I want to be his sub, actually, what I really want, if he would have me," she looked over at him and smiled, "is to be his consensual slave. You see, in the almost one year since he has been training me, I have found that deep down, I want to give myself to him, completely and totally, a Total Power Exchange. I want his mastery of me and over me."

David beamed at her and Jon smiled. "Hmm," Jon said, "but I think I hear or at least by your body language feel there is a but in there. Care to tell me what it is? I'm not a mind reader, you need to tell me if I'm to help."

Alice dropped her gaze and to Jon's surprise, blushed slightly. "I've, um, I'm twenty-six and if we marry when David want's, I'll be twenty-seven. Uh," they could see she was fighting back tears. "I don't know if I can spend the rest of my life sleeping alone. A married woman, possibly with children, sleeping alone with her husband one floor below her in his own big bed. The only alternative is to sleep on the floor at the end of his bed and that doesn't look any better." She took the tissue Jon offered her, "I have lost both of my parents and the only other family member I've got. Except for a couple of friends and David, I am alone, all alone, and I can't think of a lonelier place for me to be but in a marriage-bed without my husband beside me." She sighed, "I love his rules, rituals, and protocols, I know I will thrive on his mastery of me, but being deserted like that, that scares me."

David put his arm around her and held her tight. He looked at Jon and gave him a questioning look. He knew he needed to fix this and fast.

Jon looked at Alice, "I really need a bit of water dear. You know where the kitchen is, can you get me some from the fridge. I would like to have a word with David and I'll let you know when to come back in."

Alice looked at David, he nodded to her and smiled, "just give us a minute. It'll be okay."

When she had left the room and closed the door Jon turned to David, "did you notice that what your parents did to her, the way they treated her, was not what was foremost on her mind but your sleeping arrangements were? I think you may want to tell me about this."

David grunted. "I told her that we would be sleeping in separate rooms and that if she were to sleep in my bedroom, she would be on some blankets on the floor. I said that to keep the Dom/sub dynamic it would have to be that way." Jon looked at him, surprised, "well, that is how Uncle Maurice taught me and how he lived."

"Hmm, what can I say," Jon started. "First off, your uncle, as much as I loved him as a friend, was an old-fashioned sod. Lala begged him for a child but he denied her one of the most basic and primal urges a woman can have. In fact, he canned her for nagging, pretty badly I gather."

"Just before he died," David said, "he told me that was one of his biggest regrets, was not giving her a baby, something to have of him."

"Mmm, we talked about it." Turning back to David's problem, "what worries me now is this idea that you can't keep a D/s or M/s dynamic going if the two of you sleep together. Is your vision and the thing that makes you an Alpha male so weak that a beautiful, soft body sleeping next to you will unravel everything? If it does, then you are not cut out for this at all."

Jon sat forward in his chair, "David, I think your girl is. I watched her the other night and I see the signs. Is she perfect? No, but we, none of us, ever reaches perfection. That is why, every day, we put on our Domley pants, continue to grow in our lifestyle and do the same for our sub or slave." Jon put his mug back on the tray.

"Think about what I've said. She's ready and I think you know it too, but are worried something will mess things up. Now, I would like a couple of minutes alone with Alice, if that is okay with her soon to be Master, uh, Dom."

David smiled, "I think that would be fine. I can step out and get her. If you need me, just give us a shout, I'll be in your waiting room." David took the coffee service and went to find Alice in the kitchen.

She was standing looking out at the garden from the window over the sink. Alice turned and went to David. "What happened," she said with trepidation in her voice. David only smiled, put the tray down, and gave her a kiss on her forehead. "He wants a few minutes alone with you and I told him it was okay. Now, don't worry, I will be in the waiting room and if he wants me back all he needs to do is call out to me."

Alice went back into the office and sat on the chair opposite Jon. He noted this. Hmm, closing off any chance that someone else would get close to her. "Alice, how do you feel about what you said this morning? Is there anything you would like to add or clarify?"

She sat in thought, "no, I don't think so. The part about how his parents reacted to me, well I've heard stories about how some of the other brides were treated in my dad's family and it's not that dissimilar. Oh, they weren't all but called sluts and whores, but close to it. Mostly it was the girl's fathers who were considered the gold diggers, pushing their daughters into marriages just because of the family's fortune."

"And that doesn't bother you," Jon queried?

"Well, yes, but you see, the joke's on them. They thought they were being clever by speaking in French. I don't know if it is just more comfortable for his mom and dad to do that or what, but I think they thought I wouldn't understand them. It must have been a shock to them when I told them one of my governesses had been a Parisian and taught me excellent French." Alice stifled a mischievous grin. "I can, however, understand they want to protect David, I don't think they understand the kind of man he really is." She saw the look on the man's face, "oh, I don't mean the kink, but the strength of character he has and the, well, just the way he is."

Jon smiled at her, "so, I think you're going to be just fine. Communication, that is one of the bedrock foundations of what your dynamic with David will be. Be open, let him know how you feel, and if you two ever get into another pothole, my door is always open." He stood and walked her to the door. Looking at David he smiled and gave him a nod of approval but then told him, "David, give Alice the car keys so she can wait for you, I just have a few words for you." Looking at Alice, "go along, I won't keep him but a minute or so."

She took the keys and left by the front door.

Turning to David Jon looked serious, "she'll be okay, but are you planning on having your formal collaring ceremony on the day after your wedding like your uncle did." David nodded in the affirmative. "Do you notice the way she blushes? Well, I think you need to prepare her to be seen naked by other people. Richard is having a dinner at his house in two weeks, maybe you should go and take Alice. Let her see how the other slaves and subs do things. You don't have to put her in a robe the first time, but I'm sure the others will make her feel welcome. It will help ease her into it. She doesn't have to be shown at her first dinner, but you know what the ceremony is like at the collaring, you don't want her anything but calm at that."

David nodded his head. He thanked Jon for everything and turned to go. But Jon had one last thing to tell him, "Oh, and David, you may not know it, but you have a slave there. I've never felt it that strong since my girl. Be careful with her, cherish her, and train her well."

David could see Alice sitting quietly in the car. No texting, fidgeting, or playing with the radio, just quietly waiting for him to return. "Thank you, Jon, thank you!"

David slid in on the driver's side and looked at Alice. Her serene smile and the beautiful look on her face. This is what he had always wanted, she was the girl for him. Now to fix what he had messed up without switching power back to her. She had given him control, or at least that's what she was promising, because she didn't want it. He needed to cede on the sleeping arrangements without her thinking any of his other hard limits were up for discussion.

"How long will it take for you to get your things together and check out of the hotel?" David asked her.

She gently, softly, put her hand on his and smiled up at him, "my things are already in the trunk of my car. If you will take me there, I will follow you home, Sir."

His heart lept, but he had to be cautious and do as Jon said. They would talk about it when they got home. "Uh, you know we have some unresolved issues to dispense with at home. There was supposed to be a punishment when we got home from my parents and that didn't happen. These things just don't go away you know, we need to deal with them." He saw her squirm. "Defying me is exactly that, defiance. I won't have it and you need to learn that. But we will take care of that at home."

They rode in silence back to the hotel. The valet had her car under the portico and he handed her the keys. The assistant manager stood on the steps and waived at her. David stopped his car in front of her and ran up to the woman. "I think I left an unopened bottle of champagne in my fiancé's room, could you send someone for it?" She smiled and asked him to wait a moment. Shortly a maid came out holding the bottle. "Thanks, he said" and gave the maid a tip.

Alice followed David in her car and they were soon home. He told her to put the car in front so he could take her bags in. "I want you to go to your Zen place and take off your 'outside' for 'inside'. Meet me in the dungeon when you are done.

Alice did as she was told and in about twenty minutes she knelt formally in front of David. She had the soft shoes on that was for in the house but nothing more but the cuffs and collar he wanted her to wear. David had changed into his dungeon clothes and paced around her.

"Look at me," David demanded. He paced a bit more before he stopped in front of her. "This is not about who does or doesn't pay for the wedding, but about defiance. Do you understand that? Oh, permission to speak."

"Yes, Sir, I understand." She said quietly.

"Do you have your butt plug in, show me." Alice stood and turned her back so she could thrust her butt out so he could see it was in place. "Good girl, now, turn around and present." Quickly Alice turned to face him, opened her legs wide, thrust her pelvis forward, and opened the folds of her labia so he could clearly see her clit and the opening to her core. "Who have you pledged your sex to?"

"You Sir," she said.

"Go to the spanking bench," he said with a gruff voice. "Get the blindfold on your way there."

Alice did as he wanted and stood to wait for him by the bench. He put the music on he wanted but put the remote control to the system in his pocket. David bound Alice to the spanking bench and put the blindfold on her. "I don't like to punish you, but you leave me no choice. Do you understand why you are being punished?"

Softly she said she did. He growled in her ear and stepped over to the wall to take down the cane he would use on her. This would not be a play session. This was for punishment. No ramp up or warm up, no music or ball-gag to stifle her screams. Punishment pure and simple and he hated having to do it.

"Alice, count for me." He took a couple of practice swipes with the carbon-fiber cane and Alice stiffened when she heard the whoosh it made. David delivered the first strike and Alice flinched and shouted "One" before she could recover the second, "two" he waited for the next in order to break up the pattern, not knowing when the next one would come would disorient her, keeping her from relaxing into the blows. The third, "three" and so it went until she screamed through four and five. By six she was crying, "six" she said with a whimper.

David put the cane back and looked at his handiwork. He rubbed the ugly welts that he had raised on her butt and undid her restraints. The blindfold landed on the table.

He wrapped her in a soft blanket and pulled the remote from his pocket. Soothing, soft music gently emanated from the speakers located around the room. He picked her up and took her upstairs to his bedroom. He sat with her on the sofa in his room and rocked her gently. The music could be heard from hidden speakers in the master bedroom. Soon her crying quieted and she looked up at him.

"Did I do okay, Sir," she asked in a weak voice. He hugged her tight and kissed her forehead. After a while she dozed off. He did also, still holding his girl.

Later, much later, they sat in the kitchen where they had eaten salads from the fridge. Alice cleaned up the table and made their coffee. David sat by the fire and watched her work. She brought his mug and sat hers' down beside it. Standing in front of him she bowed her head and asked if she may say something. "Of course, you can Alice. What do you want to say."

She raised her eyes to him, "I would like to know if your mother would please like to help me plan my wedding, that is if we are still having a wedding?"

He reached out and pulled her down into his lap. "Oh my god girl, of course we are still getting married, at least if that is what you want." She nodded. "Okay then, we are, now what do you say if we call and ask her." Alice looked at the clock. He followed her gaze, "don't worry about the time, they are always up late."

David pulled out his phone and called his mom. David's father answered and cautiously asked how he and Alice were, "very good, Dad, can I speak to Mom, please?" With a laugh his father call David's mom to the phone. "Mom, Alice wants to know if you would like to help her plan her wedding?"

A pause with much shouting and laughing, he could hear his mom shouting at his father, "Alex, Alex, I have a daughter, I have a daughter!" Talking to David again, "oh my boy, I would love to help her in any way I can, a little or a lot. I'm here for her." Alice could hear everything.

Goodbyes were said and David put his phone down. "You know, you are an amazing woman. So surprising. Now, I have one for you. What do good girls get?"

Without missing a heartbeat, "They get to cum, Sir." Alice said quietly.

"Mm hm, but they also get to sleep in their Master's bed." Alice showered kisses all over his face before she slipped down to the floor on her knees.

In a formal kneel she looked him in the eyes, "does this mean, Sir, you will make me your slave?"

"If that is what you want my sweet. And my place as Master is strong enough to survive a slave-girl or soon to be slave-girl, sleeping alongside of me in my, our, bed." He saw the look of pure adoration in her eyes. Reaching out for her she fell into his arms. "If you are tired, I think you should ask if you can go to bed now."

WEDDING BELLS

Six months is not a long time to plan a wedding. Alice was finding this out as she looked at venues and the availability of the church. She had discussed the overall size of the guest list with David. They both wanted a small intimate wedding, but the size of David's family made a guest-list of over three hundred more likely. His mother stepped in to help.

Family weddings in David's family on his father's side were run off of a central list that David's Aunt Lou kept. It was computerized with all of the information that would be needed and was available to be customized and downloaded. When Alice put it on her laptop it ran for page after page, and didn't include friends or co-workers. David's mother's family was very small with only two maiden aunts, she understood how such a list of all of the Khoury family could be daunting. With the skill of a master chef she chopped, sliced, and tweaked the list down to a core group of two hundred. The friends and associates of both David and Alice would number less than a hundred.

Alice invited Cora Khoury, David's mom to lunch to talk wedding. The kitchen table was not where she would serve the lunch for two but the dining room that so far, she and David had not used. A lovely bouquet of fresh flowers was arranged in a vase as a center-piece. The good porcelain service from the stately cabinet in the dining room graced the table and Alice had polished the silver flat-wear to perfection.

Cora sat across from Alice as she ate the last of her snapper filet. "This was a lovely lunch my dear, and you made all of this," she said with a wave of her hand. "David didn't tell me you can cook." She sighed, "but then from the time he was a teenager he wasn't as close to his father and me as he was to his Uncle Maurice. Oh, I know we were busy with the restaurants and Alex also had other interests, but it seemed he just slipped into his own world. But I must say his uncle did help show him that being a disruptive and disrespectful teenager was not going to help him and his grades improved as well as his study habits. It wasn't all bad."

"David is a wonderful man and I love him very much," Alice replied. "I hope you can see this now. Neither of us knew what the other's family had or didn't have. We are in this for our mutual love and affection."

The older lady patted her hand, "we see that, his father and I, and I want to thank you. I haven't seen my son so much in the last five years as I have these last couple of weeks."

Alice stood to put the rest of the dishes in the kitchen and then returned with the wedding planning binder and her laptop. The two women delved right in and Cora gave Alice some great tips about the venue. "My husband is a substantial donor to the Cartwright Museum in Oakland," looking over at Alice she said, "have you been there?" When the girl nodded in the affirmative, she continued. "They have that beautiful big open area where they hold events like this. I have checked with them and they have three dates open. Talk to David and between the two of you decide which you would like. It can accommodate the group we have."

Cora went on, "since your nuptials will be held in the late afternoon, we can specify no children, if you like. Most of the family will agree with it because they don't like having their small ones out after eight or so anyway."

Alice flipped to another page in the binder. "My best friend is currently studying in Italy but will come to be my bridesmaid. I don't know how many attendants we need to have, but since David is having a good friend of his from med school as his best man, I can go with just the two. The best man is also dating the maid of honor so that will make things easier."

"Alice, this is your wedding and if you only want a small wedding party, that is your wish. David doesn't have any one cousin or anything who he is close to so don't worry that someone in the family's nose will be out of joint. Go with what the two of you," she patted her hand again, "and especially you, want."

Reaching the middle of the binder Alice paused. "I think there are only two major items left." She briefly looked up at the ceiling, righting herself she went on. "I would like you to go with me to choose a wedding dress."

Cora's eyes filled with happy tears. "Oh, Alice, I would be honored to go shopping with you! All of my life I had wished I'd had a daughter or daughters along with my son. I dreamed of what it would be like to help her have a glorious wedding."

"Wonderful! I have arranged with David to go to New York this weekend to shop. We will have three days and I've made appointments at three of the best bridal salons. My designer, Kami Worth, is also going so if the dress we get needs any adjustments, she can see to that. Also, we will have the use of a private residence while we are there so no need to worry about getting in and out of hotels." Alice flipped to another page.

"The last item is one I hope you will agree to. Uh, all of this," gesturing to the wedding binder, "is a lot to do. This is not going to be a small wedding on a beach somewhere but something a lot bigger and I want to have a professional touch as in a wedding planner. There would be control over things like food, I think your idea of a venue is great, but I'll talk to David, flowers, colors, and etcetera."

Cora thought for a moment, "I think you are right. Going from place to place trying to find just the right thing will take up time and I don't think we can afford to use that time shopping." She reached for her purse and opened it. Cora pulled a delicate little cherub out of her purse and set it on the table. "When we have a wedding, the guests usually expect a 'favor', something to mark the occasion, to take home with them. This is a sample a lady who does these for a living in our family makes."

She handed the favor to Alice. The delicate little porcelain ceramic figurine was of cupid. His sash had David's and Alice's names in script and on the bottom, the place to put the date. It was blue-tinged white and was outstanding." Alice was very moved. "I will show it to David and see what he thinks, but I like it, very much."

The two women chatted for another few minutes when his mother stood and said she should go. "I will email you the plane reservations for New York and we can pick you up for the airport in the limo." Said Alice, "we will also be going to dinner the two nights while we are there so you might want to pack accordingly."

They hugged at the door and David's mother left as a very happy future mother-in-law.

Later, much later that afternoon, David came home to his lovely, naked girl in the kowtow position waiting for him by the front door. Hearing his key in the lock, Alice sighed and thanked the universe for her man and her place in his life. She only hoped the universe would continue to smile upon her.

On the next Saturday after they would return from New York, David was taking Alice to Master Richard's party. David had RSVP'd the invitation a week before and for the last several days was preparing Alice for what a M/s, D/s party among his circle of Masters and Doms would be like. "I'm sure you will do fine, there is nothing to worry about. We will be in the company of friends and no one there will judge you, but your behavior and attitude will reflect upon me so I need to prepare you for this."

Alice was on a cushion in a kneeling position in front of the chair where David sat by the fire in the kitchen. Her eyes were on him but her hands rested, palms up, on her thighs and except for the collar, cuffs, and soft shoes, she was naked. "Yes, Sir. I understand."

David played with one of the strands of hair that had fallen from the loose braid she wore. "In our house, you are naked when we are alone. How does that make you feel? Do you feel comfortable with this."

Alice thought about it and didn't like where this conversation was heading. "I'm okay with being naked in the house because it is what you want and I understand your reasons for it. I'm not ashamed of how I look, I spend some time and energy trying to keep my body in shape so there is nothing to be concerned about."

"Alice, when the Master/Doms of my group meet for a dinner in a private house, most things are no different than an invitation from a friend or business collogue. Master Richard has an excellent dungeon in his home and after dinner there will probably be couples playing. Sometimes there might be a demonstration like the one we attended a few weeks ago at Master Morris's home. Just like when we play, the sub or slave will be naked for the most part. Does any of that bother you?"

Alice blinked and asked, "are we going to play?"

David leaned down and kissed her on the forehead, "no my pet, I would not play with you on the first time out. We are not yet formally bound by a contract and I wouldn't have you do something like that until we are, and maybe not even then." He could see the tension leave her shoulders.

He went on though, "the Masters and Doms will be served by their respective sub or slave at dinner and if we have coffee and brandy after we eat. The subs and slaves will eat after the men, in the kitchen. Not every house does it this way, but that is how Master Richard runs his house so we do it like that for him out of courtesy." David didn't see any negative reactions from Alice so he forged ahead. "In some houses the dress is formal for the dinner, but in Master Richard's, it is more casual. After the dinner, when the guests move to the dungeon area, the subs and slaves change into dungeon wear. For our group it is a short robe that is see-through, has slits up the sides, is open in the front, and has a tie belt. That is all a slave or sub wears except if the owner wants her in heavy collars and cuff so they can play."

He'd been watching her reaction as he told her all of this and at the mention of 'see-through', a look of horror registered in her eyes. Seeking to reassure her, he said, "you would not be asked to wear such a robe when we go there. I just want you to be aware of what will be happening." He put his hand on her shoulder and fell a slight tremor.

"Why, why would they want their subs or slaves naked for all to see? I don't get it." She said in a strained voice.

He reached down and pulled her into his lap. "Alice, each one of those men are proud of their girls. For the women there is no body shame that keeps them from being seen by others. Think about people in a nudist group, it's not a sexual thing, but a life-choice to not wear anything. For slaves and subs it shows they're comfortable enough in their own bodies, and life, to be seen by anyone in the group, in fact they are proud of who and what they are. Other Masters and Doms never touch or try to interfere with another man's girl in any way."

David stroked her hair and held her tight. "David," Alice began, "are you ever going to make me do that, go without clothes and let people see me?"

"My sweet girl, I will never do anything until you are ready and you want it. When I tell you we have much work to do before a collaring ceremony, this is part of what we need to achieve." He felt her stiffen. "The dinner at Master Richard's will only be the first of many events you will attend with me between now and your collaring."

David continued to rub her back. "There is also a possible collaring ceremony coming in three months' time. Master Donald is taking his sub as a slave at their recommitment ceremony so you can get a look at what your ceremony will be like after our wedding." She turned her face to him, he kissed her lips and continued. "Each ceremony differs depending on what the Master wants, with input from his girl of course, but most of the ritual and protocols are similar."

"Did your uncle do the same with Lala? Was she made to go naked in front of other people?" A slight shiver went down her spine as Alice talked.

"Lala did it because she was proud of being my uncle's cherished slave. To her it was a badge of honor that she would serve her Master and that he was so assured of her that he wanted to show her off as his most prized possession." David said to her as he tried to sooth the tension from her.

"What was her ceremony like, I mean, what did they do?" Alice asked.

David held her close. "You should ask Lala, I was only an observer, it was her and my uncle's ceremony. Only she could give you the kind of answers you seek." He pulled his girl around so he could kiss her. "Write to her and let her tell you what it was and meant to her."

They sat together, watching the fire until late. David had no early appointments, he wasn't on call, and no surgeries were scheduled. Finally, he decided it was time to go to bed. Alice, as she had been directed to at the beginning, asked permission to go to bed. Giving her permission, David also whispered in her ear, "prepare yourself my love, I will use you tonight."

With a light step Alice went to prepare to be inspected and the wetness between her legs just continued as she replayed his last words to her.

Several minutes later, poised in the inspection position, Alice waited for David to come to the bedroom. He had been as good as his word and the second closet was filled with her clothes as well as her Zen spot where she could change her 'outside' self to her 'inside' self anytime she had been away from home and David. Soon she heard him walking into the room.

Alice arched her back and pushed her butt up so David could do his inspection. She was very wet having thought about him and the possibilities of what he might do to her. She craved this, wanted this, and wanted him to see that she was ready for anything.

David checked the butt plug. It was the second largest one, Alice having become looser with using the first two. He turned it and Alice's body immediately reacted. Next, he checked how wet she was and found her pussy practically dripping. Such a good girl and when he put one of fingers in his mouth, she tasted good too. A sharp smack on her butt cheek got her attention. "Stand," he growled. Alice bolted upright. He turned her to face him.

One hand went around her waist to hold her, the other hand grabbed a handful of hair and pulled her to him. His mouth came down on her and their tongues battled for control. Alice relinquished control immediately. Her arms were around him and the hand he had use to steady himself then went to her nipples.

First one and then the other of her nipples turned to sensitive buds in his fingers. A moan of pleasure escaped from her. He pulled his mouth away and said, "breath, Alice, breath." Then his mouth again claimed her. He picked her up and put her on the bed. Shedding his clothes onto the floor he began caressing her as he joined her in the bed.

"Open," he said as his hands reached her thighs. Parting her legs, he could see her sex and with one finger began to caress her. She took her hands and was about to grab his hair. "Stop, hands above your head."

David got off the bed and grabbed a tie that was hanging on the open closet door. He bound her wrists together above her head and secured them to the headboard. Looking at his handiwork he whispered, "tonight you are mine."

He put himself between her legs and again stroked her labia until the folds parted and her clit was exposed. His tongue replaced his finger as he licked and sucked her. His tongue darted in and out of her pussy and he rejoiced in her wetness. His hands worked both breasts and nipples, pulling at the nipples, squeezing, and pinching them.

"Open your eyes my girl, I want to see your lovely eyes," he whispered. "I will tell you when you can come my sweet." His tongue went back to work on her clit. He felt she was near, but not yet, he wanted this to last for as long as possible. He drew away from her sex and adjusted his position. His cock was hard and ready for her. He slipped the knot holding her to the headboard and he released her hands.

Sitting on the edge of the bed he turned her to sit on his lap facing away from him. With his legs together and hers' straddling him, he lowered her down onto his cock. "Not yet pet, not yet." David had purposely left the closet door open so the full-length mirror was in front of them. "Open your eyes Alice, watch us, watch us."

The two watched as his cock disappeared into Alice and then reappeared, sliding out almost completely and then returning to her wet, hot, velvety lushness. She used her hands to brace herself as they watched and fucked. David took his thumb and slowly circled her swollen clit. Alice tried to speed his rhythm but David insisted on going slow.

She was beginning to zone out from the intensity of her desire to cum. Every time she was close to the edge, he would remove his thumb and continue only the in and out of his cock. Beads of sweat formed on her upper lip and her thighs began to quiver. David still kept her on that knife's edge without letting her tip over into an orgasm.

"Alice," David whispered, "I want you to begin circling with your hips. Slowly make one rotation and then stop. I will tell you when to make your next circle." She did as she was told. He cautioned her to slow down and she did, moving at a snail's pace. "Good girl. Now, begin again and remember to stop when you finish one rotation."

Alice concentrated on the movement of her hips and it helped her to keep control of her desperate need to climax. David again used his thumb to circle and tap on her clit. It was building again, the urge to cum but still she was pulled from the brink. Alice wondered how David could keep from coming himself but too much brainpower used to think about his predicament meant she might mess up and cum leading her to disappoint David.

Suddenly, David lifted her off of him and set her down on the bed, "all fours, now," David commanded. Quickly she took the position demanded of her. He pulled her to the edge of the bed, "wider" was all he said, indicating she needed to open her legs more. He pulled her onto his cock and the slow in and out of his fucking started to go faster and intensify. His hand again found her clit and the strumming of her clit with his thumb increased.

Now he was ready for her to cum and his thrusts got harder and faster. "Cum, pet, cum for me." David pulled her swollen clit as he pounded into her. She had reached the top and exploded into a raging orgasm. Over and over, it rolled through her like thunder with a loud bolt of lightning at the center of her core. She felt David fill her with the hot cum she had been craving. When he was finished, he continued to stimulate her clit for one more orgasm. David took his girl and lovingly laid her on her side of the bed where she could sleep. Covering her with a light blanked, he bent down and retrieved the tether used to bind her to the bed. Crawling in beside her, he pulled her towards him and they lay spooning, sleeping until dawn.

New York

James Henry had been the Blake's family driver until the death of Alice's mother. When he left the family's employ after her death, the limousine he had lovingly cared for those many years went with him. He was semi-retired but when Alice called, he assured her the car was in top condition. He would take her party to the airport for their trip to New York.

The airline's first-class lounge was only partly full when Alice and her small group took comfortable leather seats near the floor-length windows with the expansive view of the airport stretched out below. The attendant brought coffee and the tea Kami Worth, the designer, requested. A commotion at the door and Alice saw David striding into the room.

Alice saw David and rose from her chair, "David I" he cut off her words as he embraced her and kissed her. When he finally let her breath again, she said softly, "I didn't know you would be here!"

Looking deep into her eyes, "you didn't think I would let my love go to New York alone, did you?"

Alice shook her head, "no, I guess not, but you can't go dress shopping with us."

He laughed, "little Alice, I've got some shopping of my own to do." He greeted his mom and was introduced to Kami. Leaning into Alice he whispered, "besides, I want to use you tonight." David could feel Alice's reaction to his words and knew he had made her wet in anticipation.

Their flight was soon called and they were able to board. A small breakfast was served but David and Alice, sitting side by side, opted for just coffee and juice. The trip from the sunny Gulf Coast to an equally sunny but colder New York passed quickly.

As Alice and her group exited the terminal, a group of mostly men dressed in plain dark suits stood with signs bearing various passengers' names. Another, almost ancient man in full chauffer's green livery stood apart from the rest. He held no sign but seeing Alice he came forward, "Miss Alice? Miss Lucinda has sent me to get you."

Alice recognized the man as Dillard, the driver for their hostess, Lucinda Rose Hubert. To her fans of the 1950s cinema, she was known as Lucy Rose but to Alice she was simply Aunt Rose. They would all be staying with her on Park Avenue.

At the curb a vintage Rolls Royce had a promeninat place within the group of limos and town cars. A porter brought the luggage which Dillard stowed in the boot. The three women got in the back seat while David sat facing them on a jump seat next to the pull-down bar.

The building where Aunt Rose lived was a pre-World War II Art Deco edifice which had morphed from apartments to condos in the 1960s. Each floor was one unit except for the penthouse which took up the last three floors. The doorman, seeing the old familiar car arrive at the curb, was quick to open the door for the passengers. The luggage was taken out and set on a cart to be taken up by service elevator. The doorman waited until everyone was inside the lavish resident's lift before unlocking the button which would take them to their destination.

As the door slid open, the light from the floor-to-ceiling windows made the foyer one seamless part of the large living room ahead of them. A petit lady, probably in her late eighties, was sitting in a small wing-backed chair near the center of the room.

"Welcome! Welcome Alice!" the woman said in a lilting voice. Looking toward a fast-approaching middle-aged woman dressed in a black servant's uniform, "Tilly, bring my great-niece and her friends over here where I can look at them."

Alice took her great-aunt's hands and leaned down to kiss her. "Auntie Rose, thank you for letting us stay this weekend."

"Nonsense girl, this old place belongs to you. No use you going to some hotel, I still have your parent's room and it's ready for you." Rose turned to look at the others. "And who do we have here?"

David came to stand by Alice and as he slipped his hand into hers' she said, "Aunt Rose, this is my fiancé, Dr. David Khoury," then motioning David's mother forward, "his mother, Cora Khoury, and uh," motioning to Kami, "and Kami Worth my designer."

Aunt Rose's eyes lit up, "My, my so our little girl is getting married! Your grandmother and parents would be so pleased! So why are you here and not at home planning a wedding?"

Alice sat down on the chair next to her aunt and motioned for the others to also find seats. "I'm here to buy a wedding dress, that is why my designer is here and Mrs. Khoury. David, well David says he has his own shopping to do," Alice reached over to David to hold his hand.

"Wonderful!" Rose said, "Tilly, Tilly," she shouted for the housekeeper, "take everyone to their rooms." Looking back at Alice, "I suppose you'll be sharing with David," Alice nodded. "Put my niece and her fiancé in the Camilla Suite. Oh, and tea is at four."

Next to the elevator which had brought them to the penthouse, was a very ornate-grilled private elevator which would take the guests to the third floor where the bedrooms were located. In this condo, the first floor was servants' quarters, utility rooms, and a gym. Second floor was public rooms, kitchen, office, library, dining and morning room, and a full suite which was used by Aunt Rose.

When the elevator stopped at the third floor, the four people fell into line behind Tilly who put Cora Khoury in the Violet Room and Kami in the Daisy Room. Alice stood before the door with the word Camellia on it and lightly touched the name. Looking at David, "mother loved camellias. When she died, I wanted them for

70

her casket but they were out of season." Tilly opened the door to the Camellia Suite for David and Alice. Minutes later Tilly brought their luggage and wished them a pleasant stay.

David turned the key in the lock on the door and took Alice into an embrace. His mouth claimed hers as his tongue took control over her. His hand deftly relieved her of her blouse and after unbuttoning the skirt, he slid the zipper down so it would pool on the floor. Alice kicked the skirt away along with her shoes. She stood before David naked.

"Alice, you always take my breath away with your beauty!" David was shedding his travel clothes as he eyed his girl. "I want you on that bed, now, I'm going to fuck you until you can't come anymore!"

Alice scampered to the bed and got on her hands and knees. David had other ideas and flipped her over onto her back. "I want to eat your sweet, sweet pussy first and after that I'll decide what's next." He positioned himself between her thighs and used one shoulder to push her legs further apart. His hands were pulling and pinching her nipples. Alice moaned with each tweak of a nipple.

Suddenly David got up and opened one of his bags. From it he pulled a red sash. He bound Alice's hands together and raising them above her head, secured them to the headboard. A black blindfold was put over her eyes.

David resumed his licking of Alice's sex. His fingers teased her nipples and his tongue parted the folds of her labia to allow him access to her clit. He flicked it back and forth then started a slow circling movement. One hand left her breasts and using one finger, he entered her. Angling his finger he found her g-spot and brought her close to orgasm. "Don't come until I tell you!"

She could hear the passion in his voice and hungered to suck his cock or give him pleasure. But he had her bound and at his mercy as he brought her to the edge but then would pull back before she could tip over into an orgasm. Finally, when she was sure she couldn't take anymore, David growled, "come Alice, come for me." The orgasm which had been building deep inside her began to break when she felt David move over her and plunge his rock-hard cock into her.

David slipped the knot on the sash and her hands were free. "Finger your clit, I want at least two more orgasms out of you!"

Alice found her clit and furiously circled and tapped her clit into another orgasm while David continued fucking her wildly. "I'm close Alice and I want at least one more from you, give it to me baby, give it to me!"

"Fuck me David, fuck me!" Alice cried as a massive orgasm from her met David's climax. She felt him pumping his hot cum into her as he ripped the blindfold from her. He slowed and rolled them onto their sides with his cock still inside of her. They could feel each other's hearts racing and then start to beat at a more normal rate.

David smoothed a tendril of Alice's hair from her forehead. "Hi."

"Hi, uh, welcome to New York?"

David and Alice lay in each other's arms and talked. "Tell me about your Aunt Rose," David began. "Why did she say this is your apartment?"

Alice snuggled down into David's arms. "She is actually my late mother's aunt on her father's side. When she was young, she was in the legitimate theatre, which was okay since it was mainly Shakespeare, but she got a chance to go to Hollywood and she took it. Her family was furious. She came from some serious old money and they disinherited her. She did some films but then she met a director, Franklin Hubert. She was the only one who could ever call him Frankie. They got married and she quit working."

She continued, "in about 1960, Frankie Hubert died in a car crash in Connecticut. He hadn't been working for a couple of years and most of their money went in some bad investments their financial manager got them into. My grandmother told her to stay here. Anytime anyone from the family needed to be in town, they would stay here and it is part of the estate I inherited. When she dies, I'll have to decide what is to be done with it. She will stay as long as she wants."

David let out a low whistle. "I'm impressed! Any other homes or houses?"

Alice smiled, "Oh, there is a little ski lodge thing in Telluride, the trust that manages the Howard Blake Museum bought our old family home, but I manage the Trust, and there's a cottage in England, Oxford to be exact. My grandfather bought it when Dad was in college there," She thought for a second, "that's all the houses I know of, at least the ones any family ever lived in or visited regularly."

David sighed, "I had no idea. I am still so sorry for the way my parents reacted to our engagement, but I guess now would be a good time to tell you, in more detail, what they were so worried about." He paused while he pulled her closer.

"My great-grandfather, Michael Khoury, had gone to Saudi Arabia as a young man to work. He had a degree from the Sorbonne and was highly thought of by his professors. A young prince was a classmate and recommended him to his father back home in Riyad. Michael had taken his degree in architecture and architectural history."

David's cock slid out of Alice and he stopped while she licked their combined juices from him. She smiled at him when she finished then resumed her place at his side. He continued his story.

"The prince's father, being one of the younger sons of iben Saud, was very wealthy and powerful. He wanted a palace which would reflect his place in society. That was Michael Khoury's first commission. Artisans were brought in from Italy to cut and lay the stonework and still others to lay the mosaic tiles. Everything from the Venetian crystal chandeliers to the pillows on the low couches were designed by him. In the end, it was a masterpiece."

"If that had been the only commission, well let's just say he was paid quite well, he could have gone back to Lebanon a rich young man. However, other people wanted villas and palaces built. So, he and the prince who had been his classmate went into business together. In Saudi, fifty-one percent of a company must be owned by a citizen of Saudi Arabia. The company not only designed his work, but a construction company was started to build each project."

"Early on, the old prince would ask Michael about converting to Islam, but he always declined. When he was in his forties, he went to Beirut and married my great-grandmother. She was a member of the Beirutei family. If Lebanon still had princes, they would be the Beirutei family. She was also Maronite. They had the one daughter, my grandmother."

"Michael stayed in Saudi for another twenty years and was actually made a citizen. If you were to look around Riyad, Jeddah, or even Ta'if, you would see his work in stone, steel, and glass. The partner bought him out when he retired to Paris. Everything is sitting in a Swiss bank, waiting for me to claim it." David started kissing Alice, the conversation forgotten as they hungrily but softly made love.

Showered and dressed, Alice and David joined the rest of their group in the living room. Promptly at four, Tilly rolled Aunt Rose out to sit with them for tea. A girl in a black and white service uniform pushed the tea cart in from the kitchen. She served tea or coffee from the sterling silver service, then passed among the guests with two multi-tiered towers of savory and sweet treats. Small tables sat by each person so the delicate china tea service was not left to balance on a wobbly knee.

David excused himself and made the explanation he had an appointment with someone and had to leave. Aunt Rose reminded him that dinner was at eight, drinks at seven-thirty, and "oh, we dress for dinner here." David kissed Alice and whispered in her ear before he left.

When Alice returned to the Camilla Suite, she found Tilly finishing the unpacking of David's and her suitcases. "If you tell me which of your gowns you will want for dinner tonight, I'll see to it that it's pressed." Alice thanked her and taking out a book, curled up on the sofa to wait for David to return.

He sent her a text message and told her that he would text her from the lobby when he got back. Lock the door and I expect you naked. When I knock, open the door and take up the kowtow position. When I enter, I'll decide if or how I'll use you, just like at home. He had her wet just thinking about it. Half an hour later Tilly brought the cream silk dress and David's dinner jacket back from being pressed. David texted soon after and Alice prepared to greet her Sir.

She heard David's step on the hardwood floor of the hardwood outside of her door. Her position by the door to greet him made David very pleased with his girl. Raising her up to standing, he kissed her long and hard. "Go dress, or we will be late for drinks." With a playful spank on her bare bottom, she set about fixing herself for the evening. As the two were leaving the room David whispered in her ear, "I will use you tonight like you have never been used before."

David led Alice past the elevator to the sweeping staircase that would take them to the living room. Her emerald green silk dress hugged her body and if anyone would think to look for panty lines, they wouldn't find them. The built-in bra was the only undergarment she wore. Kami Worth, her designer had added an extra panel of protection to the backs of each dress she had designed for Alice and this one was no exception. Any wetness caused by David's whisper would not show.

Kami and David's mother were already in the salon. Aunt Rose was sitting in her wheelchair and was in the process of transferring to one of the wing-backed chairs. Tilly assisted her and settled her into the chair before removing the wheelchair to an inconspicuous place behind one of the camel-backed couches.

When David and Alice descended the stairs, Aunt Rose gave a big smile. "You two look like you are fresh out of the nightclub scene of the 1950s! Alice, I love that color on you and David, your white dinner jacket reminds me so much of my Frankie!" Turning to Tilly, "get everyone a drink before cook calls dinner."

David steered Alice to a sofa near her aunt and took the scotch from Tilly. Alice had a drink but Kami and Cora Khoury both declined. Aunt Rose noticed and said, "Frankie and I always had a drink before dinner and brandy with our coffee after. Neither of us smoked, but when we had guests who did, Frankie would take them outside. No one comes here much anymore so I don't have that problem."

It seemed like no time before cook called the dinner and they all moved to the large dining room and had a lovely meal of game pate', sole, and roast duck. Conversation around the table was lively. Aunt Rose finished her dessert of profiteroles. "What will you be doing tomorrow? Dress shopping?" she asked Alice.

"Mm, yes, I've made appointments at three bridal salons to see what I can find. Kami and Mrs. Khoury, uh Cora, will be going with me to choose something" Alice said. "David wants to do some shopping of his own, so ..." her voice trailed off since she didn't know exactly what he was shopping for but he knew he couldn't go dress shopping with her.

David smiled, "I have an appointment with an old friend of mine at Tiffany's."

The group left the table and retired to the salon for coffee and brandy. Kami, pleading she needed sleep, left the party and Cora Khoury was not far behind. When Aunt Rose finished her brandy, Tilly came with the wheelchair and took her to her room. "Goodnight you two," she said as she was being rolled away.

Back in their room, it took David no time to get Alice out of her dress. He then undid the strap on first one and then the second shoe, taking off each one as he did so. Rising up to his full height, he shed his Jacket, shirt, and trousers. Crossing to the dresser, he opened the bottom drawer and took out a box.

"Tomorrow you will be out of my sight and trying on dresses. I don't want anyone to look at you nude." He opened the box and took out a delicate thong and bra. Reaching out to Alice, "here, put these on, I want to see if they fit."

Alice complied with his request. The bra fit perfect and the thong covered just enough in the front but virtually left her butt naked. "You are stunning, my love," breathed David. He slipped his arm around her and palmed her ass cheeks. "I want you so bad. Take those off, wear them tomorrow, but now I have something else for you to try."

David again went to the bottom drawer and pulled a small box out. Opening it he removed a silver chain and some clips. "Come here," he told the now naked Alice.

She moved to where he was sitting on the bed. "Stand in front of me." David took the silver chain and brought it around her waist and held the two clips in his hands. One of the clips had a short string of blue crystals attached. David told her to open her legs. He attached one of the clips to a pussy lip and the other to the opposite lip. Where the two clips crossed, the string of crystals hung down over Alice's now exposed clit. "Turn around, I need to adjust this."

Alice turned and he made the chain slightly tighter. Now she was fully exposed and the edges of the crystals were in direct contact to her clit. Her nipples went hard and the areolas nubbed in arousal. "Now, walk to the door and back" David said.

Alice turned and walked to the door, turned and walked back to the bed. With each step the arousal was more intense. The crystals moving across her clit was sending shocks, wonderful shocks, through her. "So, how does that feel my love" asked David in a low, growly voice.

Alice strained to talk, finally a whisper of "I've never felt something like this. I'm just …"

David put his arm around her waist and drew her to him. He set her on his lap and opened her thighs. Playing with the crystals he said, "intense, aren't they." He kissed her and continued to play with her exposed clit. "You want to come, don't you? What if I told you I wanted you to wear this all day tomorrow?"

"Oh god, that would be torture, wanting to come but you not being there to let me." Alice sighed, "I love this but I need, want to come."

David put her on the bed. "Open your thighs for me. I want to see my lovely girl." He knelt down and, pushing the crystals aside, used his thumbs to circle and tap her clit. Alice cried out. David took a long finger and put it in her cannel then crooked it to massage her g-spot. "Come for me my sweet girl, come for me." He held the crystals aside with one hand and he began licking her clit with his finger still inside of her. Alice exploded. Her back arched, hips came off the bed, and her thighs quivered. After the first orgasm he pulled two more from her. By this time her clit was swollen and when the crystals again fell upon it, the feeling was beyond intense.

David pulled her into his lap and hugged her. "I don't know what I will do without you tomorrow." He pulled her up to the top of the bed then took off his underwear. His cock sprang free from the fabric. Alice loved seeing him fully erect. It was long, thick, smooth, and straight. He fit her perfectly. He nudged her thighs as far apart as they would go. Pushing the crystals aside, he entered her.

Alice raised her head so she could see him fucking her. His hands traveled to her breasts and kneaded her, pulled her nipples, and bent down to lick at them while he was making love to her. "I want to fill you with babies, drink your milk, and then put another in you. I want sons and daughters like you." His rhythm increased as did the ferocity of his thrusting. The crystals were between David and Alice's clit, sending her over the edge more than once. With an uncharacteristic bellow, David filled her with his seed then collapsed as he rolled them both so she was on the top and he on the bottom.

David pulled out of her and grabbed his phone. "Open your legs, I want a picture of the cum oozing out of you." He snapped a couple of pictures then showed them to Alice. "I want to do this to you every day and night. Do you think you would like that?"

Alice looked at him and whispered, "that is my dream."

Carefully, David removed the labia clamps and put the items back in their box. "I want you to wash these tomorrow, but right now, I want to inspect you before we sleep."

Alice got into position and with a firm slap on her ass cheek, David told her to put on her cuff and attach herself to the rope he had put on the bottom corner of the bed. They slept in each other's arms.

Breakfast was eaten early and the women went with Dillard in the Rolls to their first appointment. David's appointment wasn't until the afternoon so the driver and car stayed to take them to the next shop.

The first bridal salon had some lovely gowns but Alice didn't like any of them. She was looking for a particular style and 'mermaid', princess, and some design bordering on slut just didn't do it for her. Dillard took them to the second shop but it was no better. They went back to the apartment for a light lunch and then to the big bridal salon in the afternoon.

David joined the women in the Rolls and Dillard dropped him off first before taking the ladies to their last appointment. The woman assigned to them had pulled several gowns to show Alice but once in the dressing room, took them and excused herself. "None of these are right for you. Please give me about five minutes, I have a gown that will be perfect."

Alice sat in her underwear, the set David had her try on the night before, and waited. A slight knock on the door and the black-clad woman came in carrying a silk dress bag. She hung it on a hook and turned to Alice, "I had to get this one from the vault. It is a one of a kind and, well, you just have to see it." She undid the silk bag and slipped it off of the dress.

Alice gasped, the dress was a striking white silk satin that was so simple it was elegant. A scooped neckline was caught on one shoulder with a lace and seed-pearl inlay. The long sleeves ended in scallops while the gown flowed into a short court train. The woman helped her into the dress and went to find a veil to go with it. Alice stood on a small raised platform and looked at herself in the mirrors that lined the room. It fit her like a second skin and would only need to be hemmed. She loved it. This was her dress.

With a veil on her head, Alice walked out to where Kami and Cora Khoury were sitting. Both women clapped when they saw her. "Oh my, that is beautiful," Kami said. With her phone, she snapped a photo to show the dress to Alice's Aunt Rose.

Cora was crying happy tears. "I think you found your dress. David will be so happy!"

Kami went back to the dressing room and helped Alice out of the dress. A floor manager came to talk about the price. Alice handed her a credit card, the dress was to be sent to the apartment by the end of the day, and champagne was brought in to toast the soon-to-be-bride.

Kami left the group to go to a store, Mood, where she wanted to shop and buy for her design studio. Cora and Alice got in the Rolls and Dillard drove them back to the apartment building where her Aunt Rose lived.

On Sunday morning Cora Khoury attended church in a nearby Orthodox Church and David and Alice prepared to leave. It was a very productive trip to New York. David got what he wanted, his parcels would be shipped to his home address, and Alice got the dress she knew was right for her. Kami had her purchases from Mood shipped because everything wouldn't have gone into her suitcases.

Their afternoon flight back home was uneventful. Aunt Rose told them all how nice it was for them to visit. At one point she pulled Alice aside to talk. "I want you to take this, Frankie gave it to me when I finished my last picture," she put a flat box that was closed by a clasp in Alice's hands. "This can be your "something blue" for your wedding."

Alice opened the case and lying on a velvet bed was a beautiful necklace of sapphires and diamonds. Alice shook her head, "this has to mean so much to you, I can't take it."

Her aunt insisted. "Alice, you are my only living relative that has ever had anything to do with me. When my father and mother died, I was never mentioned. You are my heir; I'm just giving this to you a little early. Take it, wear it, and know that in spirit Frankie and I are there with you." Alice put the case in her bag. David would see it on the day they were to get married.

With the trip finished and a dress bought, things at the old house could get back to normal. David added the labia clips he had used on Alice to his toy bag and she was again naked in the house except for the old collar and cuffs David had her wear. The party of David's lifestyle friend, Master Richard, was going to be that weekend and she needed to prepare herself.

RICHARD'S

Master Richard's party was just days away and Alice was worried about it. She had received the reply from Lala about her collaring and if David wanted the same for her, it meant she would be, at some point in the ceremony, naked before his group of Masters, Doms, and their respective slaves or subs. These were some of the same people she would be meeting at the party on Saturday night.

Standing before the full-length mirror in the master bedroom closet, naked, she wanted to make a through assessment of what she looked like and what others would see. Her height was above average for a woman at five foot nine and the color of her hair was brown with red-tinged highlights. The length and color of her hair weren't going to be changed, David liked her the way she was so that had to be left alone. She turned to the side to see how her naked breasts looked and decided they were okay. Like every woman she felt she could lose five pounds, but that couldn't happen before the party. Hmm, she would ask David what needed improvement.

Resplendent in the collar and cuffs she wore in the house, it was time for her to fix dinner. The small locks which affixed the leather on her wrists, ankles, and around her neck make a not unpleasant clinking sound as she walked form the bedroom to the kitchen. The fire in the kitchen burned low and Alice made a mental note to put more wood on so it would be as David liked in when he got home.

Dinner was going to be simple. She had shopped that afternoon but after the rich fare in New York, she thought something less formal would be best. Salad, some basmati rice flavored with a bit of chicken stock and spices, with sautéed chicken breasts in a shawarma flavored cream sauce, and roasted brussels sprouts for a vegetable. Everything was ready for David to walk through the door.

Alice's phone pinged with a message that David would be home in about five minutes. Checking the food and fire, Alice took her position by the door. While she waited for the sound of his key in the lock, she ran through some of the rules she had memorized.

- The submissive or slave will keep an open mind.
- The submissive will communicate honestly and openly with their Dom.
- The submissive will know themselves.
- The submissive will care for their mental and physical health.
- The submissive is acting with free will. She has asked to be a submissive with full knowledge of what that entail.
- The submissive has limits that shall be respected.

Alice heard the car door, his tread across the porch, and David's key in the lock. She had to stop herself from quivering in anticipation of her most important person coming home. David saw her kowtowing to him as he stepped inside of the door. The curve of her back, her butt thrust up in the air and the butt-plug firmly in place. The hour-glass curve of her waist as it cinched in from her full bustline and then flared out to her lovely hips. This was his girl and a more beautiful one he had never seen.

David dropped his case on the hall table and put his keys near it. Turning, he reached down and twisted the butt-plug and elicited a groan of pleasure from Alice. "Stand." Alice gracefully rose, first to a kneeling position with her back straight, and from that position she rose to standing. David was pleased with how easy and fluid her movements were. His heart swelled and his cock matched the sentiment.

"I think I smell something good in the kitchen. Let's eat and then I will decide how I will use you tonight." Alice turned to follow David into the kitchen and the promise of being used kept her wet in anticipation of what Sir might do to her.

They sat quietly, eating. David enjoyed her ability to let silence sit so he could decompress from a busy day in a noisy hospital. Unlike some people, she didn't need to be constantly chattering away or spend her time in endless questions of no import. She was calm, it could even be called serene, and he liked that about her. David smiled at the peace she brought to his life.

Halfway through the meal he asked his girl how her day was. She told him about the self-inspection she had performed and asked him if there was something he would like improved about her body. "No, pet, you are just right for me. I love your full, pear-shaped breasts, the nipples centered in the dark areolas. Your waist is trim and the flare of your hips is lushes. I like how your butt is just the right size and oh so spankable. There is nothing I would change because you were made just for me and you fit me perfectly." She smiled at him and then he wondered what had brought this about, the conversation on her body. "Tell me pet, why the worry about your body?"

Alice laid her fork on her plate. "I, uh, received a letter from Lala today. I'd asked her about her collaring ceremony and she gave me, uh, all of the uh, details."

David questioned. "Oh, I see. And what is it that she said that started this question of if there is something I want changed on you?"

"Um, yes, it was the part in the ceremony where her robe is removed and, well, everyone is there and can see her. Then she is secured to chains and her legs are opened so your uncle can put his brand on her thigh. I understand the pain it would cause, but all of her, everything, can be seen by everyone. And all of this, the day after your uncle takes her as his wife." She looked down at her hands in her lap. "Is this what you will be wanting, me displayed for all to see? Your bride with nothing to cover her nakedness?"

David could see the look in her eyes. Master Morris was right when he said she needed to be comfortable naked around the group of Masters, Doms, slaves, and subs who make up the group he belongs to and who would be witnessing his girl's collaring. He would have to think about that. He didn't want to do something which might be too much to soon, but there was a timetable for this to happen and it wasn't that far away.

"You are perfect in your body. Every day you are naked in this house with nothing but those old leather cuffs and collar to cover you. These people, most of whom you will meet at Master Richard's dinner party, will be the guests and witnesses at the collaring ceremony when I will officially give you my collar and accept you as my slave." He waited for a moment before going on. "When you asked to be my sub and then my slave, do you know what you are asking when you said you wanted me to take you as a consensual slave?"

Alice softly answered, "yes, Sir, I think I do." She continued to look at him. "Lala added a copy of the contract, the Master/slave contract, she had signed with your uncle. I've read it and if it's like what we will sign, I understand what it says."

"I didn't know she still had a copy, but I'm glad you read it because ours will be similar but with a few things that pertain to how I want things to be and with maybe some different hard limits for you." David went on, "do you remember that the first part of the contract talks about the slave, which will be you, does a TPE or Total Power Exchange with her Master which is me. You will be giving me total power over you. If I want, I can decide how you wear your hair, what clothes you will wear, when and if I want you naked, who I will allow you to talk to or be around. Total, 24/7, full-time, three hundred sixty-five days a year." She was listening intently to what he was saying. "The second part of that contract says that, and I stress this, that as your Master, I will be responsible for your health and welfare. That means both physical as well as mental health."

He took both of her hands in his, "Alice, my sweet, sweet girl, I will never ask anything of you I don't think you are ready for or can't handle. In a few days we will go to Richard's and you'll get to see how the other subs and slaves in our group handle wearing the robes and it may help ease your mind some. I'm never going to hurt you but that doesn't mean I'm not going to push your boundaries when I think you are ready even if you don't think you're there yet."

"Now, something I do want you to do is look at the new rules I will send you. The ones you have are for a submissive but since you have asked to be my slave," he caressed her cheek, "my dear sweet slave, you need to learn the new rules. They are different so read and learn them carefully. If you have any questions, you know communication is a high priority so ask and I'll tell you what it all means."

"Since it looks like we have finished our dinner, wash up, and meet me in the dungeon. I've missed playing with you while we were away."

Entering the dungeon, Alice was surprised to see David with his cellphone in his hand. One of David's strict rules was there was no place in a dungeon for a cellphone. She saw him lay the phone face down and she assumed the position by the door that she would normally be in when David came home. She waited there for him to see her, or approach, or give her a command.

David strode to the door. "Up girl. I want you on the Cross with a blindfold." Quickly, she got up, went to the cabinet where the blindfolds were held, and choosing one, made her way to the cross. She put the blindfold on and waited for David to give her further instructions. Reaching out with his strong hands and long fingers, her moved her into position and fastened the cuffs to the St. Andrew's Cross so she had her back to him and was spread-eagle.

Alice could hear him move around and the sense of anticipation began to go to work on her. At one point he leaned in and breathed in her ear, "tonight is about me." Just his voice, as low as it was, made her even wetter. She could sense him putting things out to be used on her and not knowing for sure what they were, her mind went to all sorts of places.

Finally, David started the music playing. The background and tempo for this night's use of her was a single obo. The haunting sounds of the reed instrument was beginning low with a decided tempo and if his taste in dungeon music was anything to go by, it would progress into a more rapid and manic sound before it was done.

She heard the 'woosh' of the flogger flails mere microseconds before it touched her flesh. It was a soft flogger, probably the doe-hide one he was so fond of. He was warming up and was starting easy. Alice knew it could go anywhere from there.

Alice was leaning into the flogger and enjoying the pain/pleasure aspect of his play when he changed to a gally whip. He began by laying down stripes from her upper thighs to her mid-back, one upon the other until her back looked like it was a not-unflattering horizontal stripped material. He paced around her, whispered in her ear, and the music, the lonely sound of the obo, kept time to his work.

David laid the gally whip aside and rubbed both of his hands up and down his handy-work. He knew Alice had dropped into subspace by the way her head lolled to one side. He took the single-tail whip and popped it near her ear. Immediately he saw her tense and her head begin to straighten. Before she could come fully out of her happy place he began with the whip. A moan escaped her lips and he gave her one last strip to go with the others. Putting the single-tail down, he walked up behind her and taking one of his fingers, ran it along the seam of her sex.

Ever so slightly he used his finger to part her pussy lips and was greeted by proof of how wet she really was and how aroused the play had made her. Before the music could crescendo, a full orchestra joined in to take the lone obo to the end of the piece of music. David released his girl from the St. Andrew's Cross and cradled her in his arms. A tendril of her hair escaped the braid she always wore in the dungeon and he smoothed it back for her. He fished the remote from his pocket and silenced the music. Wrapping Alice in a blanket, he carried her to the bedroom. He would lock up and clean his toys in the morning.

While he held her, he removed all of the cuffs and collar from her except the one she would need to bind her to the bed. As she began to rouse, he gave her a bottle of water but continued to hold her. This was his girl; his most beautiful and precious girl and the emotion brought a tear to his eye. There was one more hurdle to get over before the wedding and an official collaring. If she couldn't do this, if she didn't trust him enough to do this for him, was that a sign that she wasn't really giving her power over to him? If she couldn't bring herself to be naked during the collaring ceremony, would he have to let her go? He held her close and muffled his sobs in the blanket.

The morning of Master Richard's dinner party a package arrived addressed to David. Since Alice was not expecting anyone, she slipped on a shift dress she kept in the closet in the hall before she answered the door. An older man in a well-known delivery service's uniform asked her to sign and she took the parcel.

When David texted Alice about an hour later, she prepared to meet him at the door. The parcel was on the hall table. She heard David unlock the door and he told her to rise. Seeing the package, he told her to take it and put it on the bed in their room. She came back to find David still standing by the door. "On your knees and suck it," was all he said.

Sinking down to her knees, Alice unzipped his pants, freed his hard cock, and proceeded to pleasure him. She loved doing this to him almost as much as he enjoyed receiving the ministrations of her mouth and hands. Her juices were wetting her thighs by the time she finished licking the last of his cum and she put him back in his pants. "Rise, pet, I have a surprise for you."

Alice followed David to the bedroom where the package was laying on the bed. "Open it," was all he said. In the box, protected by layers of tissue paper was a midnight blue silk dress. Alice took it out and held it up. It didn't look like anything she had ever worn and her puzzled look made David laugh. He took it in his hands and held it up to her.

The skirt was short and pleated all round. The top, well she guessed it was supposed to be a top, was draped from one side of the front to the opposite side in the back. David looked at it and told her to try it on.

She slipped the skirt over her hips and pulled it up to button it. One button, hidden among the pleats, was the only thing holding the skirt together. She stuck one arm through the top part and David help pull it around so it fit. Her ample breasts were settled within the drape at the front and the material went around to the back. There would be no way to hide the fact she was braless and if she were to bend over, it would be equally plain she had no panties. Looking at it she realized it was a modern representation of a toga.

David ran a strong but delicate hand over her skin and her nipples hardened. The silk was no match for their arousal and it was clear by the hard points, she was aroused. David pulled her to him and claimed her mouth. His tongue overpowered her and she melted into him. He ran his hand up under her skirt and a finger along the seam of her sex. She was wet and her thighs glistened with her juices when he looked under her skirt. David breathed, "take it off."

He released her and she slipped the garment off and hung it in the closet. David took her hand and pulled her to the bed. Pushing her down, he began stripping off his clothes. Rock hard abbs, a result of workouts in the hospital gym, and strong arms were bared for Alice to admire while she waited for him. The rest of his things landed at the foot of the bed when he joined her. He resumed kissing her as his hands caressed her, tweaked her nipples, and squeezed her ass.

One hand found her seam and rubbing it, parted her pussy lips and found her clit. She could feel his erect cock against her hip and reached out to caress it and take it in one of her hands. David was always too big around for her to use one hand and when she tried to shift so she could use two, he pinned her down and took her hands in one of his and raised them above her head. "This will last love, this will last."

"Leave your hands above your head," he demanded while he moved down to lick her clit and use his tongue to dart in and out of her canal. He took two of his fingers and crooking them against her g-spot inside of her, he continues to use his tongue to flick her clit or suck it in between his lips. She was close, he could tell by the spasms in her vaginal canal against his fingers. "Don't cum until I tell you," he whispered in between licking and flicking her clit. He slipped a third finger into Alice and then pulled all of them out to slow down before she came.

He moved over her and slid his cock in. He heard her breath catch and the moan that elicited. Slowly he moved in and out, in and out. The rhythm slow and purposeful. "Take your fingers and pleasure yourself." One of her hands dipped between them and he could feel the movement as he slid in and out. Again, she was close, he could feel it in his cock the way she tightened and he felt the pulsing in his core. He was also almost to climax but he wanted her to have at least one orgasm before he took his pleasure.

"Come, pet, come," he groaned. Alice exploded, shattered all around him and he felt it in his cock as her wet sheath squeezed and pulsed against him. "Augh! I'm coming Alice, I'm coming!" David shouted as he let loose in bursts of cum that filled Alice and slid out of her as he continued to pump his seed into her. He wasn't finished with her yet and his fingers replaced hers' as he circled and tapped her clit into another orgasm. Sated, they lay in each other's arms, drifting off to a restful sleep.

Showered and changed, Alice put on the dress David had bought her to wear to the dinner party at Master Richard's. She had a pair of strappy sandals that went well with it. She waited for David to see her before she finished fixing her makeup. Alice had put her hair up in a soft bun but it didn't look quite right to her. Turning from the mirror, she saw David watching her. "Do I look okay or should I do something different?" she said.

David came and stood behind her. He removed the pins from the bun and let her hair fall naturally to her shoulders and down her back. "I love your long hair, wear it down tonight." He reached into his pocket and pulled out a small box that Alice recognized from New York. "Turn around, I want to put this on you."

He knelt before her as she raised the short skirt of the toga. He fastened the clips to the lips of her labia and adjusted the silver chair that went around her waist. He snugged it tighter so the blue crystals were directly in contact with her exposed clit. David used one of his long fingers to move the string of crystals to the side while he kissed her clit. "Mm, you taste like honey," he breathed as he let the crystals hang again over her clit.

Standing in front of her again, he looked at the effect the clips had on her nipples and noticed they were hard and pointed under the silk of the dress. "Walk around for me, I want to see how well you respond to the stimulation."

Alice walked into the bedroom and then back to the bathroom where David was standing. Each step or movement made not just the crystals but the fabric of the skirt brush against her exposed clit. Shock waves of pleasure shot through her and into her nipples which were hard and aching under the folds of the toga. The silk fabric, although smooth, were their own kind of sensual torture. If David's plan was to keep her on the edge of orgasm for the rest of the evening, he couldn't have chosen a better combination.

She stood in front of him. He tweaked her nipples and felt the hardness. "You are so beautiful when you are aroused my sweet. I don't know if I want anyone to see you like this. Perhaps we forgo that particular piece of jewelry for tonight. I have something else that may be better. Come with me." David took Alice by the hand and led her into the dungeon. He sat her on the sofa and rummaged through the cabinet where he kept the cuffs, clamps, and other small items.

David had two boxes in his hands. Setting them down, he opened one and removed a silver chain, he knelt and fastened it around Alice's ankle then took its twin and put it around her other ankle. Opening the second box he took a heaver chain out and put it on her wrist with a second chain on the other. "There, these represent the cuffs you wear in the house. When you go out, you will wear these when the leather cuffs will not be appropriate. If we have guests in the house who are not lifestyle, you will wear these. I don't ever, from this day forward, want to see you with out either the leather or silver cuffs."

Alice bowed her head and whispered, "yes, Sir."

"Come then, let's go." David led the way out and Alice waited by the front door while David locked up the dungeon. She loved her chains and was proud to wear these tokens of his coming ownership of her.

The ride to Master Richard's house only took about twenty minutes. It was a large home in a wooded area. The driveway and street were filled with several cars and David found a parking place across the road. The weather was mild but David had insisted Alice bring a wrap with her to ward off any chill there might be by the time they were ready to leave.

Master Richard's slave/wife elsie was standing by the door and greeted David with a deep curtsy and after asking permission from David, a sisterly hug for Alice. Alice put her purse and shawl on a chair before following David into the main room. He took Alice by the wrist and went up to each Master and their slave or Dom and their sub and greeted them before introducing Alice to them.

Alice tried to remember all of the people she was introduced to but David told her she would soon learn who everyone was. The women were in the kitchen and elsie was happy for their help. Feeding such a large group was not easy and everything had to be perfect. Dinner that night would be buffet style and the Masters and Doms would eat first, as was custom.

All of the food was put on the dinning room table and Alice was surprised at how many different dishes there were. A glazed ham fresh from the oven and a roasted-turkey were the center of attention but side dishes of mashed potatoes, peas, green beans, stewed apples, and sweet potatoes were also there. A dressing with chestnuts was said to be Master Richard's favorite. A huge salad sat in the middle and was surrounded by several small plates. Bigger china plates were stacked on a side-board along with napkins, silver flatware, and some condiments.

Several smaller tables had been set up in the den in the form of a square with an open center. Chairs from the dining room and extra chairs were waiting for the Master and Doms to sit and enjoy the company of their peers. The slaves and subs spent their time refilling glasses or taking empty plates from the table. When the men had finished. A coffee urn was produced with plenty for them to take an after-dinner cup. Once the men were settled with their coffee, the slaves and subs ate, cleared up everything, and worked until all traces of the meal was gone from the dining room, den, and kitchen.

When they had finished, elsie took the women to two spare bedrooms where they could change into their dungeon wear. Alice wasn't changing but she went along to see what it was. David had given a very accurate description of the robes each put on. Alice also noticed that for these women to be naked or virtually naked around each other was as natural to them as if they were in elegant gowns.

When everyone had changed, elsie led them out to the den where their respective Dom or Master was sitting. There were cushions on the floor for the slave or sub could kneel or sit, depending upon their Master/Dom's request. The whole scene was one of peace and naturalness. The men didn't leer or stare at any woman but his own. Quietly the women took their places on the cushions and waited for a signal from their Master or Dom to move to the dungeon Master Richard was so proud of in his house.

Alice had noticed that Master Phillip and his slave louise were not in attendance and thought she would ask David about that when they were alone. The conversation the men were having was about a recommitment ceremony for Master Donald. David had mentioned that they would attend it in another two months and the men were talking about some of the work he was asking of them. When a Dom or Master of this group had such a ceremony, it was his right to ask others in the group to help him. As Doms and Masters in their own right, that was the only time they would bend to the will of one of the others. It seems Alpha-males were like that.

At a signal from our host, Master Richard, the men all got up and accompanied by their slave or sub, made their way down a flight of stairs to the dungeon. Basements were not common in this part of the country and the wall of windows we passed before getting to the door of the dungeon showed that it was more of a walk-out affair.

A large, sparkling pool was visible from through the floor to ceiling windows.

The dungeon had no windows but was very large and had plenty of seating space and several pieces of furniture specific to a dungeon. In the center was a double-sided St. Andrew's Cross, a couple of bondage tables, and three different spanking/fucking benches. A set of stocks stood at one end of the room and two cages, one standing and one laid on its side were at another end. The floggers, whips, canes, manacles, chains, ropes, and other items hung by hooks along the wall. Above were tracks where pulleys, hooks, and chains were found.

David found us a seat where he could sit on the couch and I sat on a comfortable cushion on the floor at his feet. He played with my hair and put my head to rest against his leg.

The first couple who wanted to session was already getting started. The girl was probably in her mid-thirties and her Master was nearer to fifty. He removed his shirt and was well muscled. She removed her robe before he secured her to the Cross in the center of the room. Her back was to us and to him. From his toy bag he took a stiff-flail flogger, a couple of paddles, and a cane. He had chosen native drums for his music.

He started with the paddles, first a slapper paddle that was made of leather but then switched to a wooden one with the name of his slave, Suze, burned into the wood. The flogger came next and the welts it rose were much different than the paddles. The music was building and he took the cane next. He began with a series of taps, starting out gentle but getting harder as he progressed. Her head began to loll to one side so that by the time the whip was cutting the air before hitting her butt or upper thighs, she was in subspace. When the music ended, he put her robe around her and took a blanket to wrap her in. He sat cradling her, whispering to her, and giving her little sips of water when she was coming around.

The second and final couple headed to the bondage table. She removed her robe and laid down on a pad which had been placed on the table. He attached her cuffs and collar to eyebolts positioned on the table or the legs and took a flogger from his bag. He played the flogger over her breasts and pussy. At one point everyone could tell she was highly aroused and was seeking release. He bent down often and whispered in her ear and each time, the arousal would subside before he began again. Finally, he grabbed a nipple in one hand and spanked her exposed sex with the other. "Come slut, come." She bucked and pulled against her restraints as she orgasmed. When it had subsided, he also took her from the table and wrapped her robe around her before taking a blanket to sit with her on a sofa. They kissed and he beamed. "Who's my good girl, huh, who's my good girl."

David tapped Alice on the shoulder, he was ready to leave. Dutifully, Alice stood and David thanked his host. Master Richard's slave walked with them up the stairs and found Alice's wrap and bag. Alice thanked her and asked, "where do you get your robes? I think I might want one." David heard what she said and smiled while elsie told her of a woman who makes them. She gave her the phone number.

In the car, David took Alice's hand and kissed it. "Do you really think you will be able to wear one of our group's robes?" he asked. "I'm not pressuring you into this you know. It has to be your decision."

Alice rubbed her cheek on his hand. "I never knew that a group of women could be all but naked in front of a group of men, especially men who are most definitely Alphas, and it was just as nonchalant as sitting down to tea. Yes, David, uh, Sir, I think I might be able to do that."

The smile on David's face said everything. His mind thought back to just a few days ago when he had feared he might have to let her go. If she could do this, wear the traditional robe all of the other subs/slaves of his group wore at celebrations or dinner parties, he saw nothing major in the way of his collaring her. She was safe, safe for him to take as his most cherished and beloved. She would be his, his to do with as he would but his to guide, care for, punish if needed, but his and his alone.

Alice watched him attentively. She could tell he was deep in his own thoughts so she held her hand in his until he would let her go. Finally, his eyes began to glisten and he relaxed as if a great, heartfelt burden had been taken from him. She smiled at him and again caressed her cheek with his hand. Ever so slightly, this gentle movement brought him out of his reverie. "Mm, time to go home my sweet. I have some things I want to do to you and I don't want to waste time!"

David unlocked the door to the house and pulled Alice in with him. He wanted her and the feeling was mutual. He took her in his arms and his mouth found hers. Their tongues battled briefly but as always, his won out as he claimed her mouth. He pulled the shawl from her shoulders and it fluttered to the floor and pooled in a multi-colored mass of spun silk. Her dress followed with the release of the one button and a gentle nudge from her shoulder.

He pushed her away from him to look at her and the labia clips she had worn all night. "You are stunning and I can tell the labia clips have done their work." He kneeled before her and moved the crystals out of the way. His shoulder nudged her legs apart and his mouth claimed her swollen clit. His tongue raked over her entrance and he sucked some of the liquid from her. David smacked his lips. And again, began sucking her clit.

Alice steadied herself by holding onto the wall above the hall table when David thrust three of his fingers into her and then crooked them to find her g-spot. She shouted and moaned. He could tell she was just on the edge. "Cum, pet, cum for me. You are such a good girl and you get to cum." At this point she came unglued and even the wall couldn't keep her from collapsing. With his three fingers still in her, he managed to grab her around the waist and keep her from falling with his free hand. Lifting her, he carried her to the dungeon.

Once inside, he carried her to the big bondage bed. David's clothes landed in a pile at the foot of the bed and he carefully removed the labia clips and put them to the side. "We'll have to clean those tomorrow, won't we my sweet girl?" Alice looked at him in a post orgasmic haze and nodded.

David replaced her silver cuffs with the heavy leather ones he kept in his drawer. He bound her spreadeagle to the bed and put a blindfold on her. Then, music to set the mood for what he wanted to do. "Think about what you will look like in one of those robes. Every one will see how beautiful you are and know how lucky I am to make you, my slave. But remember, others may lust after you, but you belong to me. You always have, and you always will."

When the music started, he put a vibrator on a stand so that hit her clit just at the right spot. She writhed and moaned, "don't cum until I tell you that you can. You need to learn control my sweet." He sat astride her, and took one of her nipples into his mouth and started sucking. With his other hand he pulled, tweaked, and rolled the other nipple so that she was again moaning loudly. She could feel his erection against her and wanted to have a free hand to stroke him and massage his balls.

"Please," she begged, "oh, please let me cum. Let me suck your cock and give you pleasure. Please, I have to cum!" She pulled at the cuffs and shouted for release. David changed sides and sucked the other nipple while his fingers played with the nipple he had just left. Alice began to quiet as her body began to let her slip into her happy place. David could see it in her eyes and he got off of her and replaced the vibrator with his hand. He slipped down and put his mouth to her clit and sucked on her swollen nub. She tasted heavenly to him!

Slipping his fingers into her, he crooked them and then told her she could cum. "Cum for me, cum hard!"

Alice let loose and he felt the constrictions around his fingers. Her pussy juices glistened on her thighs and made him want her. He undid the restraints and turned her over. Taking some of her juices, he smeared them on her anal opening. With one hand he sheathed his cock so he could use her ass. A few drops of lube would also help ease him into her opening.

Alice could feel what he was doing and had been preparing for this for weeks. She had used the butt-plugs like he had ordered and also applied the oil as per his instructions, but the initial try was painful and she shouted. David pulled back and carefully began to work his cock into her ass. Slowly and with a steady pressure, he got the end of his cock and began to push in with the shaft. The initial pain began to be replaced by pleasure.

Slowly, he went deeper and deeper. He thrust into her and then would almost pull out. After the first few thrusts, she began to feel the pleasure part of being fucked in the ass. Now, she was pushing herself back onto his cock. The rhythm became frantic as he came closer to climax. David took a hand and using his fingers. Pushed into her passage and found her g-spot. The buildup to an orgasm again had Alice begging to be allowed to cum. "No, sweet, this time we come together!" David shouted.

A few more thrusts and he began to cum. "Alice, I'm coming, I'm coming, cum with me!" He pumped his sperm into her and she exploded around his fingers. David pulled out of her, tied a knot in the condom and put it in the trash can near the bed. Turning her over, he picked her up and took her to their bedroom. He removed her cuffs except the one she had to use to bind herself to the bed and pulled a sheet over her. "Sleep, little Alice, sleep." David smoothed her hair and kissed her lips. A small moan escaped her lips.

Master Donald's Ceremony and a Robe

Master Donald and his sub jenny would have their recommitment ceremony in a week. Much had happened in the interim with David and Alice. Wedding plans were going forward as were the plans David was making for his own collaring ceremony.

The robe for Alice arrived and Master Phillip and his slave/wife louise, who had not attended the dinner party at Master Richard's, decided to have a party of their own. Alice proudly wore her robe at the party and made David was so pleased and happy.

The day after the party, however, David received a call from an old acquaintance. Avery Manolo had been the head of the group of Doms and Masters that his Uncle Maurice had recommended him to when he went to Boston to med school.

Master Avery was in the hospital in Boston and needed a cardiologist he trusted. His slave/wife linda called David and pleaded with him to come. He got the next plane to Boston.

Avery was a big man. He stood over six feet four inches and as David remembered him, he was a barrel-chested man of nearly three hundred pounds of pure, clean muscle. He had once played football at Harvard during his undergraduate days and with his Alpha personality, just his presence gave everyone the impression he was a man not to be fucked with.

When David entered his room though, he barely recognized his old mentor. Gone was the mane of black hair, the sharp chocolate eyes, and the muscled giant. Even his black skin had taken on a different shade. The hair, what there was of it, was lank and grey, the eyes were cloudy and his stare unsure. Avery couldn't have weighed more than two hundred pounds soaking wet. The shell of a man in the hospital was exactly that, a shell.

David saw Avery's doctor before he went in and the news was not good. He had also seen linda, Avery's slave/wife and between bouts of crying and pleading, she begged him to save her Master. "Please, please, Master David, don't let my Master die!" was said over and over.

When David entered his room, he was shocked at the state he was in but he knew, as a professional, he could not let Master Avery see the surprise in his face. Quietly, the two men talked. "Master Avery, I've seen the tests and scans. Your doctor has a good handle on this, I don't see anything else I can do for you but be your friend and I'll be here for as long as you need me."

The old man waved that away, "David, no more Master. Look at me, I'm barely able to speak, but I have to talk to you. Remember Damian, Damian Horace? Calls himself a Master now. Be careful. He's been talking that you owe him a life and he's going to come and collect."

David soothed the man's brow with a damp cloth. "Shush, I'm not afraid of him. He's just a cheater and he deserved being sent down from school for it. I didn't get him tossed out, he got himself up on charges of cheating. If his father wasn't such a large doner, it would have been big news, but as it was, it was hushed up."

"His father's dead, he has the money now and he is out for blood. About a year ago he bought The Arabesque. Some world class dominatrixes, a stable of high-end subs all formally trained, and a group of Doms and Masters to give guests their ultimate BDSM experience. The membership fee is over fifty grand a year and the initial fee to join is a half a mil." Avery coughed and gather himself before he continued. "He also has some heavy muscle. Big guys that wouldn't think twice about beating somebody to death."

Avery seemed to drift off. Quietly he continued, "remember Rachel, Rachel Lewis? You know her Dom put her out when he found out she had a crush on you? She blames you for not taking her to be your sub."

David ran his hands through his hair. "Avery, I never touched that girl, barely even looked at her. She was not my type and at that time I wasn't ready to take on a sub, much less her. She was a mess. She had a crush on cocaine more than anything else."

"She's with Damian. He's her Master now and she is one of his Dominatrixes. She works the girls in that club like slaves, and I'm not talking about consensual slaves either. No, you be careful, you don't want to get anywhere near him." Avery finally slipped into sleep. David stayed with him for another hour and then went to find linda so she could sit with him."

It was almost three in the morning when Avery's heart finally gave up the fight. The flat tone woke linda who began keening beside his bed. David was dozing in the lounge, heard the wailing, and helped the nurses get linda out of the room so they could take care of the body. David promised linda he would stay for the funeral.

David's trip home had to be extended for three days but since Avery didn't have family besides linda, only friends and members of the group of Doms, Masters, and subs/slaves who were in it attended the memorial service. Before the service, linda came to David and asked him to remove Avery's collar, deface the brand he'd used to mark her as his property, and place it all, along with their Master/slave contract, in a box in his casket.

Another service she asked of David was to remove the labia rings which marked each five-years of her belonging to Avery. Carefully, he opened each ring, used disinfectant to clean the empty hole left by them, and put them in a box. Linda had decided to keep the rings, not wanting to lose all that reminded her of her many years as Avery's slave.

The funeral home where the service was held was full, a testament to the many friends which had come to tell Avery goodbye. A cousin, someone Linda had never known, presented himself and asked if he could speak. One of the Masters from the group was also going to say a few words.

The cousin was an ordained minister and his eulogy recounted how his cousin had been shunned by the family because he had married a white girl. "Avery didn't have a racist bone in his body, but our family, my aunts and uncles, well, I can't say the same. They thought he was dishonoring his race by marrying a white girl, but with his wife, Linda, he found the kind of relationship of love and honor that I, as a minister, ask for for each of the couples that I marry at my church. Rest well, cousin Avery, rest well."

The Master who stood to speak was one David remembered. Master Mark was of the same generation as Avery and as it turned out, had known each other for quite a number of years. They had both served in Vietnam together, two tours to be exact, and were Marines. Master Mark and Avery had forged a friendship under fire that would forever bind them together. His telling of their story was both humorous and sad. He would miss his brother-in-arms but expected to meet up with him, 'on the other side.'

The slaves/subs of the group left to prepare the home Linda had shared with Avery. A wake was planned and they wanted everything to run smoothly. David stood with Linda at the graveside then took her home. She had asked him to look at the will Avery had kept in the safe and the place where she had lived with her Master all those years, was hers. She would give it all back just to have him again at her side.

Not long before the visitors were starting to leave, David heard a familiar voice by the front door. Damian Horace and Rachel Lewis stood at the front door. He heard Damian telling one of the Doms who was at the open door that he and his girl had only just arrived and was sorry to have missed the funeral. An unpleasant few words passed between the two men when one of the Masters took charge and let the newcomers in to see the widow.

David felt his presence before he heard him, "Well, well, well. If it isn't David! Look Rach, your old heart-throb. How's life been treating you, Doctor." The last word dripped with venom as Damian and Rachel came up behind him.

Turning, David found himself face-to-face with his old med school roommate. "Doing just fine, and you?" He attempted to keep the encounter light seeing as how they were in the late Master Avery's home and in the presence of his widow.

Damian's nostrils flared, "I don't want to hear any of that pretty boy-shit from you. You owe me and I always collect on my debts." Looking over at Rachel, "you owe her, too and something tells me she wants more than a pound of flesh from you."

David looked from one to the other. "I owe neither of you." Nodding to Damian, "you got yourself kicked out of the program when you decided to cheat with my essay. When you turned that in, the professor knew it was mine and not yours." His eyes lighted on Rachel, "I never gave you any indication I was interested in you. When your Dom released you, it was for his own reasons. If you two can't handle the past, you may want to work on that with a therapist."

Master Riley, the man who had soothed things at the door with Damian came up behind him and moved Damian off to see Linda. David put down his coffee cup, said goodbye to the man at the door, and left to go to the airport and home. He could feel Damian and Rachal's eyes on him, but it didn't matter, they were in the past and Alice was his future.

The robe clad subs and slaves filed into the darkened dungeon holding electric candles. Each took her place, in a formal kneel, before her Dom or Master. The only light in the room, except for the newly arrived candles, was a pin light that shown down from the ceiling and illuminated a small platform in the middle of the room.

Two Masters accompanied Master Donald into the room and left him standing on the stage. Two slaves in light-colored but equally see-through robes, escorted jenny into the room to kneel at the feet of her soon to be Master. When everyone had taken their place, one of the Masters handed the Master/slave contract to Master Donald which he and jenny would be signing.

Alice was kneeling on a cushion at David's feet. Back straight, head held high, she didn't want to miss a moment of the ceremony. She knew that David was planning the same or similar type of ceremony for them when he gave his collar to her. She was, as always, wet and her thighs glistened with her juices. David stood with his hand lightly on her shoulder.

Master Donald was reading the contract and after each paragraph, asked jenny if she agreed to what he had said. When he had finished reading, a small table was put on the stage and one of the Masters took a knife and nicked first Donald's and then jenny's index fingers. He dripped blood from each into a bowl then added some red ink. Mixing it, Master Donald told his girl to rise. "Do you accept all that is written in our contract and do you, of your own free will come to me and ask that I take you as my consensual slave?"

After each question jenny answered in the affirmative. "This contract, between two consenting adults, is not enforceable by law of this state or country, but it represents a pledge, based on our honor, that it will be held more sacred than any oath we have ever taken or will take." Master Donald laid the contract next the bowl and a quill pen. "It is for you to take the pen and sign if you agree."

Without hesitation, jenny picked up the pen, dipped it in the ink mixed with their blood, and signed her name. Next, Master Donald took the same pen and signed above his new slave. One of the Masters removed the table and handed Donald a rich, dark velvet pouch, giving his new slave the signal to kneel, he took a beautiful collar from the bag and placed it around her neck. "Rise slave jenny and embrace your Master."

In one fluid movement, jenny rose and saying "yes, Master" for the first time, embraced her Master/husband. Loud but polite applause was heard in the room.

Two slaves came forward and took the robe from Jenny. She stood before the assemblage naked but proud of who she was, her

Master's slave. One Master pulled the chain down that was hanging from the ceiling. He affixed jenny's cuffed hands to it and raised it until she stood with feet apart but on tiptoes. Another Master, fastened each ankle cuff to eyebolts in the floor.

Another table containing a smoking solution was brought in and put by the stage. Master Donald stepped forward wearing heavy gloves to protect him from the dry ice, water, and alcohol solution in the vessel. He dipped an aluminum block about two inches cubed in the solution and taking a set of tongs, removed it and pressed into jenny's thigh. She screamed. After Donald had counted down enough seconds, it was removed and a slave sprayed the area with an anastatic/antiseptic foam.

"It is traditional that when a man takes a slave, he canes her to impress upon her that he is the Master of her. My girl, jenny, has been with me these last ten years and in the past, she had been given eight strokes of the cane, but now she is my slave, it will be ten." Master Donald took his carbon-fiber cane and flexed it.

Today was not about playing with his slave, it was in impressing upon her the fact she was now, completely and totally his. He leaned in and whispered in her ear. He caressed her and waited until a slave applied the bandage on the new cold-brand that marked her as his. Stepping back, he brought the cane down upon her beautiful, round butt cheeks. "Say it, count it out with letters."

At first his new slave had stiffened but then obeyed her Master, "S," another whack, "L" she said on the second and on through the words, slave jenny. A strike of the cane for each letter. By the time it was finished and she was released from the chains and eye-bolts, her Master had wrapped her in a blanket and was sitting with her in his lap. Stroking her hair, whispering to her, he cradled her until the tears had dried and the pain had gone away. Finally, he carried her from the dungeon and took her home.

The description of the ceremony Lala had with Uncle Maurice was very similar but seeing it in person, Alice began to understand the depth of feeling the Master had for his new slave. David had told her they had actually been married for over five years before they became Dom and sub. This was just a progression that many people who lived the lifestyle would make in the relationships they had with their mates.

At home that night, David made love to Alice for hours before they both slipped into sleep in the early hours of the next morning.

HERE COMES THE BRIDE?

Evie Marsh, Alice's best friend since grade school and Dr. Amara Dal Bianco, David's best friend since they had served together as residents, arrived a week before the wedding. Evie stayed at her parent's house and Amara split his time between David's condo and the homier Marsh place.

Evie and Alice had always been inseparable but as Evie began to reconnect with her friend, she felt like there was something Alice was keeping from her. The first couple of days she just put it down to pre-nuptial nerves, but by the third day, it seemed like a wall had gone up between them. Evie was hoping that a bottle of wine at her parent's pool house would cure that.

She had just poured the second goblet of wine in Alice's glass. "Okay, spill, what is going on with you? I leave you for almost two years and it's like we don't connect like we used to. Tell me?"

Alice smiled as she lifted her wine goblet. "David, it's just so intense. I love him so much I'm almost afraid I'm going to wake up and he'll be gone, like a ghost or something. Everyone who has ever meant anything to me, well in my family, has gone and left me behind. I'm just afraid he will lose me." She stared into her drink.

Evie put her arms around her, "don't worry about that, my god the man chased you all the way to Europe! He is not going to ghost you. He's not the type. Amara knows him very well, he's his best man, after all. He knows David has been in love with you since you first met. He's crazy for you."

"Oh, that, maybe, but I just can't shake this feeling that something bad is about to happen. Hm, tomorrow we will go to the Strathmore until the wedding. David and Amara will stay at his condo and then we will meetup at the wedding at the Museum. It Saturday evening so that gives me a bit of time to work through this." Alice put her wine goblet down and the two girls took a swim in the Marsh home's pool.

Alice had everything she needed for the next few days. Her gown was being delivered by Kami Worth, her designer, as well as the dress she would wear Friday night at the rehearsal dinner the parents of David were giving in the Strathmore's plush dining room. She left the Shelby in the garage because the mother of Evie was taking the two friends to the hotel.

Later that night, David snuck into her room at the hotel and they spent their last night together as single people. He knew that the night of the rehearsal dinner his parents and Amara would make sure he was not near his soon-to-be wife. Besides, he and Amara were going to spend that night as a bachelor party that wasn't a party but simply two old friends catching up on the last two years since the four of them had been in Florence when Evie began her studies there.

In New York, it must have been a slow news day that Thursday night before the wedding. A picture Alice had sent her Aunt Rose was used to announce the upcoming nuptials. Rose was so proud of her niece and sent the picture, along with an announcement of the when, where, and what time of the ceremony. One of the entertainment reporters found the piece and the connection between Lucy Rose classic film star and elevated the exposure of the announcement to the top of the entertainment section.

Rachel Lewis seethed when she saw the picture in her morning paper. Slamming down her cup, pieces of the broken vessel scattered across the table where she sat with Damian discussing business at the club. "Bastard, Bastard," she screamed. "David's marrying some ugly provincial bitch tomorrow! Aggggh!"

Casually, Damian removed pieces of the cup Rachel had just destroyed and waited for her to get her anger under control. Turning to the entertainment section, he saw, not an ugly girl but a beautiful young woman. He could see what Rachel could never see about David, that he wasn't interested in the exhibitionist, out-there kind of person that Rachel was but the more refined almost untouched kind of beauty that was looking back at him from the paper.

Wheels turned in Damian's brain and a plan on how to exact his revenge began to take shape. Picking up the phone he asked a friend, member of Arabesque, if he could have the use of his plane for the weekend. The man agreed and the plane would be fueled and ready for take-off by eleven that morning. The second call was made to one of the men who lived not far from David's parents. "Just find out where flowers can be sent to a Miss Alice Blake, the girl that David is marrying on Saturday. Tell them an old family friend that can't make it to the wedding is asking. Don't give my name, in fact, don't give any name. Call me back ASAP."

Finally, Damian called his head of security for the club. "Get me a couple of your men, have them at the airport by eleven. We are going to cash in on a debt." Turning to Rachel, "get your stuff together babe, we got some payback coming and I'm sure you'll want in on it."

Alice and Evie were curled up on the sofa in Alice's hotel suite, two empty bottles of wine on the table and a third had just been opened. "Gee, tomorrow you are going to be married!" Evie exclaimed. The rehearsal dinner was over, everyone had left, and it was just the two old friends, sharing the last night before one of them would be a bride. "Gosh, how does it feel? I mean he is gorgeous as all get out and built like a Michelangelo sculpture, but, wow, having him around the house full-time, you're lucky girl."

"And Amara? He's no slouch either. How's that going by the way?"

Evie blushed, "I think he is going to ask me to marry him when we get back to Florence." She looked at her hand and continued, "he has already asked me for my ring size, well, actually, his mother asked but I know it was for him. His parents really like me and I like them, a lot. I love him, I really do, but I don't know about living full-time in Florence. I kind of miss it here."

Alice nodded, "that would be a problem. He seems to be well regarded there and I know his parents probably want him to stay. What has he said? I mean, it would really be up to the two of you."

"We've talked about it but it's just talk so far. We shall see." Evie set her goblet down, "besides, first we need to get you married tomorrow! If I have any more of that wine, I don't think I'm going to look very chipper tomorrow. How about I go to my room and the wine can go into the fridge under the mini-bar?"

"Agreed," said Alice. "I'll just ponder my own insecurities while I fall asleep. See you tomorrow!" The two girls hugged and Evie left.

Shortly after, when Alice was about to get into bed. There was a knock on the door. She hadn't changed from her rehearsal dinner dress yet. "Hm, must be Evie wanting something." Alice thought. Opening the door, "Evie, I thought you were in bed."

Two large male bodies grabbed Alice and one hand put a chloroform-soaked cloth over her mouth. "Grab something to cover her with. A woman walked into the room and took the cell phone from the charger, a coat from the closet, and picked up a bag she took to be Alice's purse. Alice's wedding dress hung from a hook on the closet door.

Rachel grabbed the dress and threw it on the floor. "Pig, she can't even pick out a decent wedding dress. We're doing David a favor." She said as Damian came into the room.

Damian, however, was looking at the girl laying on the couch. No, he could see why David would want her, but now she would be his. His to do with as he wanted and use in ways that would forever repulse David. She was his payback for a life that had been taken from him.

"Look, we need to move and move now. We need to get her on the plane and out of her before she wakes up," One of the men said. The two took Alice and made if look like they were simply helping an overindulgent woman to get home. They walked her out of the hotel by a back door and put her in the waiting car. The private jet was waiting and within twenty minutes of their arrival at the plane, they were wheels up and heading for a small airport near the club. No flight plan had been filed on the trip either coming or going.

Before the plane had left the runway, Damian sent a text message to David from Alice's phone. "I can't do this because I don't love you. Goodbye." He removed the sim card and put the phone and the card in the bag Rachel had taken from the room.

David and Amara had rather overindulged in beer that Friday night and he didn't see the text message from Alice until the next morning. He had to read it three times before the enormity of the words soaked in. Amara ran into David's bedroom when he heard the feral scream coming from his friend.

David had dropped his phone on the bed and Amara picked it up, read it, and understood the anguish in his friends screams.

Slowly, Alice began to awaken. Her head hurt and her first thought was that she had indeed had to much wine the night before. She tried opening her eyes, but realized there was a blindfold over them. She was sure she hadn't put it on, Evie wouldn't do that, and she was sure David hadn't come into her room. Then she began to remember answering the door and the flash of arms and the smell and darkness.

She pushed the rising panic down and gingerly raised a hand to her head but it wouldn't budge. She was restrained but how? The hotel bed was not setup for that and this didn't smell like the dungeon at Maurice's old house so where? A noise, she heard a noise and realized a door was opening.

"Good morning. My name is Patty and I have come to prepare you to meet Master Damian." The voice was lilting and sweet but with an edge. Alice felt the cuffs being loosened and the blindfold being taken away.

The one called Patty was dressed in a black lace waist-cincher, black stockings with a garter belt and six-inch black heeled stilettos. Her breasts were bare as well as her sex. She wore labia clamps that exposed her clit which was roughed a deep red color. She also held a riding crop in her hand.

Two other women came into the room, both naked. "These subs will bath you and prepare you to see the Master. You are to eat with him. Don't disappoint him. He is kind to those who bow to his wishes but can be quite cruel to those who would not so beware." The one named Patty turned and left.

Alice let the girls bath her, style her hair, and when it came to dressing her, she was only given stockings, a waist-cincher, heels, a collar, and labia clips to wear. Alice objected to everything, but she soon understood that the girls who were preparing her were not the ones making the decisions.

Alice had never been one to use much makeup but these girls really went to town with the lipstick. Deep red lips, a brown rouge applied to her areolas and nipples to darken them, and a red liquid that was painted on her exposed clit. They put a smokey mascara on her eye's and highlighted her eyelashes with a dusting a glitter. Alice was mortified.

There was a knock at the door and a tall, slender woman with raven black hair, leather under-bust bustier, and long black heeled boots strode in with a riding crop in her hand. "Is she done yet," she asked the two girls now cowering in the corner. One of them nodded and the woman with the crop brought it down on the one girl's breast, making her shout. "Get out and get back to your kennel."

"So, Alice, is it? Hm, you don't look like that much to me, but I guess you were the best he could find in that little backwater he was living in. No accounting for taste." The woman walked around her, striking her boot with the crop for emphasis. "My name is Mistress Rachel and I am the top Dominatrix here. Master Damian wants to see you and you will comply. He told me he doesn't want me to mark you, yet, so be aware, if you don't do as he wants, you will belong to me!"

A chain was clipped to the collar around Alices neck and Mistress Rachel led her out and down the hall. The long dark corridor was punctuated by pin lights shining down on photos on the wall. There were pictures of woman, bound and being whipped with blood running down their backs, another was of a single woman with three men with their respective cocks in her ass, pussy, and mouth. Gang-bangs, men lined up waiting for their turn at two women bound to fucking benches.

Alice turned away from the photos and saw a staircase before her. Mistress Rachel walked her up the stairs into another long hall. Here the wall was still the same dark color but the photos were not quite as disturbing. Subs on their knees with a Doms cock in their mouth or a girl on a St. Andrew's Cross with someone using a flogger on her back. The hall branched off and ahead was a set of doors with a man standing guard. As Mistress Rachel approached, the guard opened the doors to let her and Alice pass.

The room was large with a sofa and chairs at one end and a massive desk at the other. Behind the desk was a wall full of various implements that Alice recognized from the dungeon at Maurice's house and quite a few that were new to her. The man behind the desk stood when they entered the room.

He came out from behind the desk and took the leash from Mistress Rachel. "I'll take her from here. Go back to your subs. We have a full guest list for tonight."

Mistress Rachel began to object but a look from the man silenced her. She left quietly.

"I am Master Damian. You are in my club and under my dominance. I know David would not have a vanilla wife so I take it you have been trained, well, at least had some training." He pulled the chain slightly. "Oh, permission to speak." He chuckled, "at least you know you must be silent when on a leash."

"David has trained me but who are you, what is this club, and why am I here?" Alice said with rising fury and panic in her voice. "I'm supposed to be married, uh, tomorrow, us today, I don't know and he was taking me as his slave in a separate ceremony on Sunday. What is going on!"

"Enough, I'll answer some of your questions, but thank you for the information about the slave ceremony. I can use that. Now to your other questions, David owed me a debt. He owed me a life and you are the payment for that life. David sold you to me and now I am going to sell you to a man who is looking for someone just like you."

Alice heard the words, words, that cut her deeply. She didn't believe what she was hearing, he couldn't, wouldn't, why?! Then, Damian flashed a picture of him and David taken by Rachel at the wake for Master Avery. That was David, it was Damian. Her world went blank as she slipped to the floor, unconscious of what was going on around her.

Damian looked at the girl at his feet. Her picture had already been sent to one particular member of the club. An international businessman who was extremely wealthy and looking for just such a girl to add to his stable of slaves. Damian shrugged, so the man's tastes ran to the dark side of BDSM, after Damian collected the money for her, he didn't care what would happen to David's little plaything. The debt would be cleared, his revenge complete.

Rachel wanted her revenge also and if Damian left her alone with Alice, he was afraid she might mark or damage the package. He couldn't have that so put the chain back on the collar, picked her up, and moved her to the sofa. A sharp ringing of the phone brought his attention back to his desk.

"What," he hissed into the phone, "now, really? Okay I'll be right down, don't move him till I get there." Damian slammed down the phone, looked to where Alice was, and decided to leave her where she was. He locked the door on his way out of the room. Only he had a key to his private office and it was the best place to leave his package until the buyer would arrive.

Alice was only just coming back to consciousness when Damian stormed out of his office. She was not restrained and sat up on the sofa. She saw the laptop on his desk where he had the picture of David and himself at some function. Alice crept to the desk and looked at the laptop.

She searched the screen to see if there was internet. Clicking on an icon, she got to an email program and brushing away tears from her eyes, she sent an email to Evie. "Ask David why he would sell me?" She pushed the send button and deleted it from the cache.

She looked around and decided she needed to get back on the couch. Then, she saw her bag. A quick search and she found what she was looking for. A jeweler's box that was at the bottom, she opened it, and took the necklace from it. Without hesitation she swallowed the chain and pendent. A smile crossed her lips. The GPS tracker in the pendant, a precaution her lawyer had asked her to take, would lead someone, anyone, to find her.